I'LL TELL YOU THE STORY

I'll Tell You *the* Story

MORE OF

Fritz Wetherbee's

NEW HAMPSHIRE

Fritz Wetherbee

PLAIDSWEDE PUBLISHING
Concord, New Hampshire

ISBN-13: 978-0-9755216-9-4
ISBN-10: 0-9755216-9-1
Library of Congress Control Number: 2006933932

Designed and composed in Minion Pro
at Hobblebush Books,
Brookline, New Hampshire (www.hobblebush.com)

Printed in the United States of America

Published by:

PLAIDSWEDE PUBLISHING
P.O. Box 269 · Concord, New Hampshire 03302-0269
www.plaidswede.com

CONTENTS

THE TOWNS

THE PEOPLE

THE WETHERBEES

ACKNOWLEDGMENTS

I WANT TO thank the following for their support of my work and this book:

Mary Ann Mroczka, senior producer, *New Hampshire Chronicle,* WMUR-TV

Jeff Bartlett, general manager, WMUR-TV

Hearst Arguyle, for allowing me to do this book

Rick Broussard, editor of *New Hampshire Magazine,* who got this project under way

Holly Scopa, Tracey Spolter, Donna Smith, Tom Griffith and Tiffany Eddy, Chris Shepherd, Chris McDevitt, Paul Falco, Chris Orr, Ryan Murphy and the rest of the *Chronicle* gang who make my on-air job easy

George Geers and Sara Minette of Plaidswede Publishing Co.

Laura for her love, support and suggestions

— Fritz Wetherbee

FOREWORD

LIKE MOST PEOPLE who live in New Hampshire, I'm from else-where. I was raised in the heart of the South, back when rebel flags were displayed without irony or agenda. In my schoolyard, calling someone a "Yankee" was asking for a fight. By the 1980s, I was work-ing in the sophisticated "New South" of Atlanta, Georgia, so it didn't seem like such a cultural stretch to date a young woman who was a Yankee by birth, the daughter of two native New Hampshire high school sweethearts.

Little did I know.

Upon our engagement, I was quickly flown north to meet the grandfather, a prominent Granite State citizen who was living his retirement years on Ragged Mountain in Andover. In his tiny house in the woods, I was served a breakfast that included fresh-caught brook trout and beans. Papa (pronounced "puh-puh") grilled me with good humor, but the humor always seemed to be at my expense. For some reason, nothing I said sounded clever or intelligent in his presence, and I was not sure how to eat a skinny fish filled with little bones at 8 a.m. Among the litany of faux pas I committed at that breakfast table was to pronounce the name of New Hampshire's capi-tal city the way I had always pronounced the variety of grape jelly that I liked on my toast: *Con-cord*.

That's probably not the only reason Papa never granted me his full approval, but somehow I managed to marry his granddaughter anyway. Within a couple of years, she and I were invited to take up residence in the family's ancestral home in south Concord—an offer we could not refuse. Still dazed by such a big move, I paid a visit to the public library (the best way to orient to a new place) and there I encountered an audio-book cassette titled: *Speak N'Hampsha Like a Native*. In light of my earlier embarrassment, I checked it out. The author and voice of the tape was someone named Fritz Wetherbee.

I imagine most people reading this book first learned to love Fritz on his decade-long stint with NH Public Television's "New Hampshire Crossroads" or more recently as the wizened historical storyteller of "NH Chronicle" on WMUR TV, but it was this old cassette tape that made me a Fritz Wetherbee fan.

It's a short tape, but I was fixated by his voice, sometimes rumbling like summer thunder, sometimes trilling like a cricket in a well, sometimes snapping like a fresh log on a fire. Each instruction he offered was illustrated by a story of some local character who was either glorified or humbled through the use of language. Long after I forgot (or assimilated) the rules of Yankee speech, I remembered these stories. The tape seemed addressed to me—and pointed at me. The state, Fritz said, was in danger of losing its authentic voice because ". . . outsiders are moving in, in fact outsiders have taken over. New Hampshire speech is dying out. The state is awash in a sea of 'Save the Whales' bumper stickers. People have actually been seen 'jogging' on Swamp Road in Greenfield."

Such sentiments now seem so dated as to be quaint (we don't "jog" anymore, we run.), but those were common concerns back then. Papa's grilling of a young suitor at the breakfast table took on a new context. It was a hazing, perhaps, but all hazings are designed to accomplish two things: to weed out the uncertain and to initiate the determined. As a young married man with a family on the way, I was determined to belong in New Hampshire. Fritz seemed like the perfect guru, my guide into the new world I would inhabit.

I learned a few of the basic rules Fritz outlined. "Words containing the letter 'R,' such as the capital city are pronounced as if there is no 'R' in them," he explained. "In fact, you'll note that the letter 'R' is pronounced as if there was no 'R' in it," he added. But I didn't really aspire to learn the dialect. I could see the real way to "speak N'Hampsha" was not by knowing the rules of pronunciation, but by knowing some great stories.

So I got a job in local journalism and kept an eye on Fritz as he rose through his various media venues. I always paid attention when Fritz told stories, because no one, it seemed, knew more of them than he did, or told them more plainly, with no fluff or polish. He would just lay out the bones of an old tale before you and, like Ezekiel in the desert, you'd see the dry bones take on flesh and blood and come to life.

I learned about his fondness for graveyards and his love of old-fashioned 3-D images. (You can still get a free pair of 3-D glasses from him when you visit his website.) I enjoyed his travel suggestions and watched in awe as he produced his video epics on grand themes like the Mount Washington Hotel catacombs and grim bits of history like the Josie Langmaid murder and beheading.

Finally our career paths crossed. I was the newly hired and, frankly, under-qualified editor of a group of regional magazines called "New Hampshire Editions." We had a special issue on the arts planned and I needed a story on Peterborough's world-renowned art retreat the MacDowell Colony. With a little research I learned that Fritz Wetherbee had been a fellow at the Colony and had written a recollection of his time there. As quickly as I could summon the nerve, I gave my guru a call. I was the classic greenhorn editor as I stammered out my request, but he was cordial, talkative even, and said he would allow us to reprint the story. But, he warned, it was a bit "bawdy."

The story arrived and I learned that among those enjoying the benefits of the creative confinement of the Colony, along with Fritz, was composer Leonard Bernstein. According to Fritz, "Lenny" was concentrating less on his composing and more on drinking and on seducing another colonist—a young man named Peter Tauber It was a great story, but not exactly the sentimental chronicle I had expected.

I mentioned this fact to my publisher, a shrewd businesswoman who was friend to many lawyers and had a genuine phobia about lawsuits. She ordered two changes: the deletion of the name of the Bernstein's young inamorato and the removal of the term "Jesus Christ," which Fritz had used as a humorous expletive. I made the changes and finished up the magazine. As I waited for it to return from the printer I had a sense that I had finally overcome the humiliation of that breakfast with Papa. I may not be a native New Hampshireman, but I had published a story by one. I was on speaking terms with my Yankee guru. I had arrived.

The next time I heard from Fritz he was not so cordial. Why had I changed his story, he wanted to know. Fritz, you see, does not mince words, on the page, nor on the phone. In fact, his colorful writing style is deceptively spare and simple. Sentences are designed like the triangular braces on a covered bridge. Words and phrases may seem rustic or ornamental, but each one is structurally essential. According to Fritz, I had pretty much pulled out the trusses of his story and left it drooping in the river.

I apologized, hung up the phone, and somewhere in the distance I could hear Papa grumbling as he scraped the half-eaten fish off of my breakfast plate.

Ever the gentleman, Fritz has seen fit to work with me many times since that embarrassing first encounter. Ever the Yankee, Fritz has never forgotten, and the story does come up from time to time. Sometimes in public.

But I think back on those vivid characters in *Speak N'Hampsha Like a Native*, and I think of the folks who festoon all of Fritz's stories—plotters, potentates, gravediggers and scallywags, madams and mistresses. All of them somehow fall prey to words, their own or others, either spoken by them or written about them. All of them are either glorified or humiliated by this unique power of language, preserved in the Yankee dialect and in the vaults of memory. And Fritz is New Hampshire's gatekeeper to this realm. He holds the keys, he knows where the skeletons are buried, and if you want to enter, you must deal with him.

And maybe, to truly arrive in New Hampshire, you must become one of his stories.

Rick Broussard
Editor, *New Hampshire Magazine*
June 2006

I'LL TELL YOU THE STORY

THE STORIES

Native American Life

DID YOU EVER wonder just what the Native Americans in New England ate and how they prepared their meals back before Europeans arrived?

Well, the Chesterfield 1882 town history has a pretty neat description of the diet of the local tribes, including the Agawams, the Nonotucks, the Pacomptocks and the Squakheags . . . all of the Algonquin Nation.

The history says that in the Connecticut River Valley, the Indians ate mostly ground nuts, chestnuts, corn, pumpkins, fish and small animals: squirrels, mice, frogs and the like.

They cooked the fish just as they came from the river, and the small animals were roasted on a spit and the entrails were considered the best part of the meal.

The chestnut trees were regarded with great respect and small ones were protected from being trampled. Pumpkins were cut into strips and dried in the sun.

Roger Williams, the Puritan advocate of the Native American, has written that tobacco was cultivated and that the natives knew how to make maple syrup . . . probably by dropping rocks from the fire into the sap in a dug-out log of some sort.

The history also tells us that the Native Americans often set the woods ablaze. That was done in the autumn. The burnings kept the pathways by the river clear of brush so that they could move more freely.

The history says the first European settlers in the valley were surprised to find so little timber standing. This also facilitated the first farming that the settlers engaged in. ☙

Laugh, Hannah

SEEMS, BACK IN the early 18th century, a young girl named "Hannah" was captured by Native Americans and raised with the tribe as one of their own.

She was a pretty girl with an infectious laugh. And early on, Hannah discovered that her laugh was probably her best asset. The members of the tribe would say to the little girl, "Laugh, Hannah, laugh," and she would burst out in a fit of the giggles which amused everyone.

She was reasonably happy with the tribe and her life, but she had seen the white settlers and how they lived, and longed to find out about them. And when Hannah passed into puberty she decided to escape from the tribe.

One day, a woman named Martha Jackson Pendexter heard a knock on the door of her frontier cabin up in what is now the town of Bartlett.

She threw open the door to find what she thought to be a young Native American woman, begging for concealment. On second notice she saw that the girl had pale skin and blue eyes. Martha Pendexter ushered the girl in. She then looked out the window to see three Indian braves striding up to her door.

"Quick," she said, "hide here." And she indicated a large barrel of feathers in a small addition off the main room. Hannah got into the barrel and covered herself with the feathers. She put her mouth to the bunghole of the barrel in order to breathe.

The Indians came into the house saying that they had seen the young woman enter the door. Where was she?

"She is not here," Martha said, "but go ahead and search."

They went to the loft and looked under the bed. They searched the entire cabin.

At one time they rapped on the hogshead of feathers but were satisfied nothing was there but the feathers. The third brave actually shook the barrel and called out, "Laugh, Hannah, laugh."

Later Hannah said that, despite her predicament, it was all she could do to keep from giggling.

But she did not giggle. And the Native Americans went away. ☙

Durham Love Story

IT WAS THE first of the French and Indian Wars, King William's War.

During this war, the local Native American tribes were bent on destroying all the settlements in the region and sending the European settlers back from where they came.

On the Oyster River, in what is now Durham, there were an even dozen garrison houses. These were log houses reinforced with thick fences where the community could repair to when there was an Indian attack.

And in July of 1693, an attack came. The warriors were lead by their chief, Bomazeen. Bomazeen had marched south with hundreds of men from his village on the Kennebec River in what is now Maine.

In the battle, the Indians burned five of the twelve garrison houses. Most of the occupants were killed.

One of the garrisons was defended by the Drew family: Thomas and Francis, their wives and children, and Thomas Jr., with his new bride, Mary Bunker Drew. Mary was four-months pregnant.

The Indians set the Drew house afire. As they rushed out, they were either killed or captured. Mary was pulled through a window by Bomazeen himself.

The prisoners were assembled, and the weak and old were killed and scalped.

The others were marched north toward Canada. There they would be ransomed by the French.

Two days into the march, one of the women became exhausted. She was left in the wilderness to fend for herself. She died.

Days later, the marchers came to a place where most of the tribe continued east to the Kennebec and their village. It was here that Thomas Drew was sent north. But his wife, Mary, had been taken as a wife of the chief. She continued with Bomazeen to his village.

Through the autumn and winter, Mary followed the tribe. Four months later in the forest in a snowstorm, she gave birth to her first child, a son.

A year went by. Thomas Drew was ransomed by the French and returned to Oyster River.

King William's War came to an end in 1697, and the tribe from Maine came to Portsmouth to smoke the peace pipe.

Thomas Drew was there, too, looking for Mary. He asked all the Native Americans he met if they knew of her. No one did.

Then he began to sing. We don't know what song it was, but it was a song that Mary had loved. Thomas sang it and waited.

And then from a young Indian maid he heard the melody sung softly.

He looked. It had been four years and she had assimilated the Native American ways; but yes, it was Mary.

Neither spoke, and Thomas left.

Within a few days a ransom was negotiated and Mary and her child were returned to her home on the Oyster River.

Despite the peace, the Indian Wars were not over and during their lifetime Oyster River was attacked many times.

But Thomas and Mary survived to have fourteen children. The couple died within two days of one another. Thomas was 93 and Mary, 89. They were buried next to one another in the same grave. ❧

The Stocks in Colonial Times

WE HAVE ALL seen or heard about the stocks, those wooden contrivances used in Colonial times for punishment of those who broke the law.

But did you ever wonder what kinds of crimes it took to be sentenced to the stocks?

Turns out the *Hollis Town History* has a listing of the laws for pre-Revolutionary New Hampshire, with a list of the punishments for particular crimes. Turns out, I for one, would have spent some time in the stocks.

Now the stocks were usually located on the town common. There were stocks where you had to stand up and your head and wrists were held in place. And there were stocks where you sat and they held your ankles.

Either way, the goal was humiliation. Your friends and enemies could come by and say things to you . . . throw rotten fruit even.

And, of course, there were the whipping posts, too.

In Hollis, if you cursed or swore in public, you were fined a shilling. If you didn't have a shilling, you were sentenced to the stocks for two hours. For more than one profane oath at a time, you got a fine of one shilling *and* time in the stocks.

For drunkenness, oh my, it was *five* shillings or *three* hours in the stocks.

For defamation—I guess that's gossiping—you could get 20 shillings or (again) three hours in the stocks.

For stealing from a garden or orchard it was up to the judge; either a big fine or the stocks or both, or, if you stole a lot of apples, it was flogging. But it was at the discretion of the judge.

OK, now we get to the really bad stuff. If you were insolent or violent to women on the highway—yeah, that's what the law says, "on the highway"—it was whipping not exceeding ten lashes. For a second offense, the culprit was branded on the hand.

And finally, for larceny the guilty person had to give back triple the value of what he had stolen, pay a five pound fine, and be whipped not more than twenty lashes. If the culprit couldn't pay, he was sold for a term of time fixed by the discretion of the court. Slavery! Wow!

Jeez, put in the stocks for swearing.

Remember the Nixon tapes? Imagine Dick Nixon in the stocks. ❧

The Widow Dennett

IN WHAT USED to be the town limits for Portsmouth . . . back in the early 1700s . . . back before they built the bridge there, only three houses were on the other side of the pond and river. They called that section Christian Shores. No one knows where the name came from, but there you have it.

One of the homes on Christian Shores was the Dennett Mansion, also called the Beehive 'cause it was big and roundish. Here lived the Widow Dennett.

The Widow Dennett had been born Lydia Waterhouse and was first married to a Captain Colby who was employed by Sir William Pepperell. When the captain died, she married Ephraim Dennett . . . and then he died.

The story is that the widow was a very competent person. She raised sheep and carded, spun, wove, and dyed her own wool and made a good living.

One day Widow Dennett was in her yard by the spring washing wool. She was wearing a leather apron, pants, and a man's broad-brimmed hat when a stranger on horseback rode up. He dismounted and asked the way to Widow Dennett's home.

The widow indicated the front of her mansion and while the man rode around and tied his horse up, she hi-tailed it to the back door where she went inside, put on a dress and answered the door.

The man was John Plummer of Rochester, widower. He had come a-courting.

He had heard of her good reputation, he said, and would ask, in proper time, he said, for her consideration of him.

They married that year and the widow moved into her new husband's home in Rochester. The two were happy, it is said, for the rest of their lives. They both were over ninety when they died and are buried side by side in Rochester.

It was never said, however, how the widow explained the guy who was washing wool outside her home that day. ☙

Dogs in Church

BACK IN COLONIAL times, the first meetinghouses were cold and drafty places.

Here in New England people came to church with firearms. That was because of the threat of Indian attack.

The weekly meeting was the one time the entire community got to see one another. It was the only day of the week when there was not back-breaking work. In fact, as the Sabbath, it was against the law to do any work.

People came to meeting with blankets and quilts in the wintertime. Some carried tin boxes with coals from the fireplace which they put at their feet.

The sermon was often over an hour long.

There was always a person with a hardwood pole with a feather on one end and a knob on the other. It was his job to awaken anyone who fell asleep. If the culprit were old or female, he'd tickle the person under the nose with the feather. If the sleeper were a man or a younger person, they'd get a rap on the back of the head.

In the wintertime, often a parishioner would insist that his horse be allowed inside. That was not uncommon in the early days when the first meetinghouses were virtually barns anyway. But as the churches got fancier, the community passed laws against bringing horses into the sanctuary.

The *Hampton Falls Town History* notes that the town voted a law that amerced a fine of five shillings "upon any person who shall ride or lead a horse into the Meetinghouse."

There was a fine of ten shillings for any person who used tobacco in the meetinghouse. The history tells us that this had more to do with preventing fire than with the sin of smoking.

Seems kinda silly to me to disallow smoking a pipe and allowing the box filled with coals in the pews.

And finally, people often brought their dogs to meeting. The dogs would warn if there were Indians in the vicinity.

But often a couple dogs would get inside the house and there would be a dog fight in the aisle. The congregation loved the respite from the sermon, although they pretended to be scandalized.

In Hampton Falls, there was actually a church officer called the "dog pelter," whose job it was to stand at the door with a cudgel and beat back any cur that tried to enter.

The history tells us that instances of extreme cruelty were recorded against some of the dog pelters.

And that often a dog would, by mistake, be beaten into the church instead of out of it. ✒

The Oldest Paper Mills

THE OLDEST PAPER mills in New Hampshire still in operation are the Monadnock Paper Mills, Inc., in Benningon.

These mills came about because of the weaving industry in the 18th century.

See, nearly all the towns on the Contoocook River were settled by Scots Irish immigrants in the early 1700s. Back then, the Ulster Plantation in Northern Ireland was under the penal saws of the British and the Church of England.

The Scots as Presbyterians had been settled in Northern Ireland by Great Britain. The fact that it was called Ulster Plantation shows that the north of Ireland had been thought of exactly the way as had the Virginia Plantation or the Plymouth Plantation; that is, a place to settle and conquer.

But by the 1700s, the English were persecuting not only the Irish but the Scots who had settled in Ireland as well. In fact, in 1703, Queen Anne required all officeholders to swear allegiance and take the Sacraments of the High Church of England. As a result, the first of the great emigrations occurred.

One of the centers of the emigration was the New Hampshire town of Londonderry, named, of course, for the place the settlers had left. Also, Antrim was named for the city in Northern Ireland. And the Presbyterian influence can still be seen there. The town church in Antrim is not, as most New England Churches are, Congregationalist. The Antrim Church is Presbyterian.

So the first Scots Irish migration came to Londonderry, and from there went on to Antrim and Peterborough and Hillsboro.

All over America, the Scots Irish settled in the thousands. In fact, a full 13 of the presidents of the United States trace their ancestry to that Scots Irish migration. Jackson, Polk, Andrew Johnson, Buchanan, Grant, Arthur, Cleveland, Harrison, McKinley, Wilson, Nixon, Carter and Bill Clinton, all come from Scots Irish stock.

But back to our subject.

Before the cotton revolution, linen was the most popular fabric, and Ireland had the greatest linen industry in the world. The Scots Irish who settled New Hampshire grew flax. During the Civil War, it was impossible to get cotton, and the flax industry was revived in New Hampshire.

Enter a man named Moody Butler.

In the early 1800s, Moody came from Ireland and settled in the section of Hancock that is now known as Bennington. There he started an industry which made use of the flax left over from linen-making. Moody beat the fibers in a vat and made high quality paper from it.

By the great falls of the Contoocook River, he built one of the earliest paper mills in the state and, as I say, the oldest one still in operation.

The mill has changed hands over the years and it has also changed its method of operation, too.

Later it made paper from linen rags instead of linen itself and, still later, it made paper from wood pulp.

In 1948, an Englishman, Gilbert Verney, purchased the mill. Verney's son, Richard, is president of the company today.

Nowadays, the company makes technical papers for medi-cine . . . for filters . . . for sandpaper . . . for industrial uses and for maps and charts.

Computer companies have used Monadnock paper for annual reports, a governor for Christmas cards, and a president of the United States for invitations to his inauguration.

The company, in fact, has the reputation for making the finest book and graphic-arts papers in the whole of America. ♠

Walpole—18th Century

THE TOWN OF Walpole was one of the social centers of New England in the 18th century, and there is a wonderful description of life before the Revolutionary War in the Walpole history.

The description is contained in a letter to the *Cheshire Gazette* written in 1826 by a Mrs. Watson, who remembered going to church in Walpole when she was a girl. Here's what she wrote:

"Mr. Leavitt, the minister, like other clergymen of that day, wore a large wig, full powdered, and when he entered the meetinghouse, the whole congregation rose.

"He, in his turn, responded with a formal bow. Powder was not worn on the hair by those who were contented with the use of the eel skin, which was considered as adding dignity to the wearer, in proportion to the size and length of the queue."

An eel skin, by the way, was a manner of braiding a man's hair so that it stood out and up from the back of the head. The braid pattern looked like the skin of an eel.

Illustrations of the schoolmaster Ichabod Crane show him with an eel skin. The longer the queue, the more important the man. Ichabod Crane directed that upon his death, he should be buried with his eel skin sticking out of a hole in his coffin.

"In church," Mrs. Watson wrote, "the officers of the Militia wore cocked hats. Of the ladies, Mrs. Leavitt the parson's wife, took the lead in dress. At church she wore a full suit of brocade lute string, which is a silk fabric. She wore no bonnet but held a fan to shade the sun. This was the fashion 'down country' which is to say, Boston.

"Next to the minister's wife sat the daughters of Colonel Bellows and their two half-sisters. They wore plain Quaker bonnets of black silk. To improve their figures, the ladies quilted their petticoats with wool, to make their hips show off. This contrasted to the smallness of their waists which were painfully compressed with long stays.

"The fabrics varied. There were homemade durance (a fabric of wool that looks like leather), and camblets (which is silk and wool), and serves which were covered with needlework flowers.

"Hand-knit stockings and high heeled shoes with buckles were indispensable.

"And it was thought an improvement to beauty and elegance to expose the petticoat in the front with an apron covering, which allowed the gown to swing open. The hair was combed all back leaving no curls or ringlets about the face.

"And finally, instead of following the modern fashion of covering the back part of the head, bonnets were much pitched forward so that the cap and back of the head was exposed."

So there you have it, life in Walpole in the 18th century. ✏

Gilman Ladd House

SECOND ONLY TO Phillips Exeter Academy, the American Independence Museum is, perhaps, the best known place in Exeter.

In this museum are two drafts of the United States Constitution, a portrait of George Washington and artifacts of the Colonial time unmatched anywhere. No wonder Exeter hosts many Colonial encampment recreations and is visited by Revolutionary War fans from all over the country.

The museum is located in the original Ladd House, which was built in 1721 by Nathaniel Ladd and is of brick. The wooden exterior you now see is either an addition to the original house or a wood facing put over the bricks.

Nathaniel's grandson Simeon Ladd was, according to one history, the president of what was called the "Nip Club." This was a society of men who gathered at a local tavern in order to sample and comment on various spirits.

As you can see, the man was a character. He kept a ready-made coffin in the house "just in case" he or someone else might need it. And Simeon came close to needing it more than a few times.

Like Icarus, he invented a pair of wings which, he said, would enable him to cleave the air like a bird. One day he appeared in an upstairs window wearing the wings and announced he would fly. Thereupon he stepped out and fell to the ground. The history does not record his injuries. Perhaps he was just back from the "Nip Club" and was so relaxed that he broke nothing.

The second family to occupy this house was the Gilmans. The family boasts two governors and a U.S. senator. The most famous Gilman is Nicholas, who was the treasurer of the colony during the Revolution.

John Taylor Gilman was the New Hampshire governor at the turn of the 19th century. He lived to be 76 years old, and the story goes that the night before he died, he was carried downstairs to his living room to say farewell to his family. There he gave full instructions as to his burial and how he wished to be remembered. He insisted his family should not wear mourning for him. "Spend upon the living," he said, "not upon the dead."

As he left the room he turned and said, "I have no disposition to leave this precious circle. I love to be here surrounded by my family and friends." He then gave his blessing and said, "I am ready to go and I wish you all, Goodnight."

He died the next morning. ☙

The Old Boar

THIS STORY IS about one of the first families to settle in the town of Hollis, a story of Captain Peter Powers and his wife, Anna.

It takes place in 1735. Back then, subsistence farming was what most families did in the Granite State.

Most families had cows and oxen, chickens and geese, sheep and pigs.

This story, in fact, concerns pigs.

Pigs, in case you didn't know, are pretty smart creatures. Many families back then just let their hogs roam free, eating acorns and rooting what they might find in the forest.

For protection of the swine herd, most farmers would allow one male pig to grow to old age. The other pigs were slaughtered when they were young and their meat was tender. But the old hog would grow tusks and become fierce.

Should foxes or wolves or bears threaten the other pigs, the old boar would come to defend them and, more often than not, prevail.

Well, on a certain day in autumn, Anna stood in the doorway of her cabin listening to the sound of her husband's ax as he felled trees in the forest. And then she heard a terrible sound, a scream, and pitiful crying.

It was one of the pigs in the forest. Something was killing one of the herd.

Almost immediately the herd came rushing from the woods, into the clearing, and across into the woods on the other side. After them came the old boar. He was grunting and gnashing his teeth and was covered with blood and gore. He leapt the fence in a single move, ran through the cornfield, and into the woods beyond.

Everything went quiet. And for an hour it remained so. Soon Peter came from the woods with his ax on his shoulder. As he approached the cabin, he suddenly stopped and listened.

Off in the forest he heard a noise.

"Anna," he said, "Anna, bring me my gun and ammunition for I fear the Old Master himself is worsted." And, turning back to his wife, he said, "Look to yourself," and he bounded into the forest.

Following the sound he traveled about a mile. He came to what is now Silver Lake. Halfway down the shore he heard a great commotion directly across the pond.

Holding his gun and powder over his head, he made his way across the water and onto the opposite shore. Just into the woods he came across an area that was matted down. Here the branches of the trees were broken and stripped, and there in the center was the old boar. At the edge of the clearing he beheld the largest bear he had ever seen.

The boar was bloody . . . but so was the bear.

Peter took aim, but the bear moved away into the woods and he could not get off a clean shot.

The boar, usually aloof and skittish around Peter, now approached him and, like a dog, showed him the first affection of his life. The boar then lay down on the ground by the man's feet and panted and groaned.

Peter shot the weapon off to make a great noise so as to keep the bear away. He made a fire and examined the old hog's wounds. They were terrible. The beast was unable to move his hind legs. Nonetheless, the old hog faced the direction where the bear had gone and stomped his forelegs as if to say, "I am still up for a fight."

Peter built the fire up and went home.

The next day he and Anna went back. The old warrior was still there, mired in its own blood and unable to walk. They put the animal in a cart and took it home.

They then went into the forest and found the large sow that had been slain by the bear, the pig whose cries had brought the old boar to the fight. But nearby they found something amazing. It was the carcass of another bear. There had been two bears, and the old warrior killed one; he had injured the other bear severely, and ran it off.

And what happened to the Old Hero? Well, he was pampered and fed and allowed to sleep and get fat.

But this was life on the frontier and, in the end, the old boar was killed and eaten . . . and as the history tells us, "Thus he helped by his death to promote that existence to the family which he could no longer do by his life." ❧

Throat Distemper

IN JUNE OF 1735, a diseased hog was slaughtered in Kingston. From that incident, the people of the time believed a great pandemic plague was created.

The disease was called simply "throat distemper" or "throat ail." Like the influenza that would strike America 185 years later, it took as its victims mostly young people.

The *Hampton Falls Town History* notes that before the disease was checked, it had killed a total of 114 persons in town, mostly under the age of ten years. In the greater community over the next year, over 1,000 people would die. Lieutenant Joseph Bachelder and his wife lost all their children, thirteen in all.

Only two houses in the entire town escaped the epidemic.

The first child to catch the disease died in three days. A week later, another family some four miles away lost three children in three days. Of the first 40 persons to catch the disease, all died.

The symptoms were high fever and a putrid sore throat.

In August the malady had reached Exeter and by the next month it had reached Boston. In October it had taken hold of Chester.

No one knew how to fight it, but the disease finally ran its course. Within two years, it had abated.

The throat distemper was to return again nine years later. At that time it killed 43 people in Hampton alone.

Later this disease, this "throat distemper," was diagnosed as probably a virulent form of diphtheria. This particular strain is acknowledged in textbooks as originating in Kingston, New Hampshire.

A note here. The only physician in 1735 to claim to successfully treat the disease was also from Kingston. He was Doctor Josiah Bartlett, who, not incidentally, was to go on to become one of the signers of the Declaration of Independence.

Dr. Bartlett treated the disease with Peruvian bark.

Other physicians of the time ridiculed his method as silly. But who knows? ✒

The Rediscovered Bones

IN THE YEAR 1850, workers were repairing the South Road in Portsmouth near the cemetery when they unearthed a human skeleton.

It took a little detective work, but it turns out the bones belonged to a man from Hampton Falls who was hanged nearby some ninety-five years earlier. The man's name was Eliphaz Dow.

His story is in the *Hampton Falls Town History*.

Eliphaz Dow had a neighbor, Peter Clough. And the two men had had some dealings with one another and had fought numerous times. Over the years they became bitter enemies.

On the evening of December 12, 1754, Eliphaz was visiting his brother, Noah Dow, at Noah's farm in Hampton, when Peter Clough happened by. The two men fell into a heated argument (although the history doesn't tell us what the fight was about).

To make a long story short, Clough invited Eliphaz to step outside for a fist fight. Eliphaz complied, but as he passed the doorway, he grabbed a hoe that was leaning against the doorway. He swung the hoe and connected with the side of Clough's head and Clough died instantly.

Later, the constabulary arrested Eliphaz. He was brought before the Honorable Meshech Weare, who had him locked up in the jail in what is now New Castle. In February, the Supreme Court indicted him and he was tried and convicted of murder. The sentence was hanging to be carried out March 20.

But Eliphaz Dow had many friends in Hampton Falls, and they petitioned Governor Wentworth to grant him a pardon. The Governor refused, but did issue two reprieves.

Nevertheless on May 8, 1755, a gallows was constructed on South Road near the town pound. Around midafternoon, a cart bearing the condemned man rumbled up the road.

The hanging was swift and was carried out by the Sheriff Thomas Packer, who had conducted many other hangings nearby.

As the deceased was a condemned murderer, he was not allowed to be buried in the cemetery. Rather, he was interred right beside the gallows in the fork in the road. There he lay until discovered by the road crew 95 years later.

The body was then re-interred in the cemetery in an unmarked grave. ✒

The Ox Towns

GENERAL JONATHAN MOULTON came from Hampton.

That was back in the eighteenth century, and General Moulton was a friend and drinking buddy of Governor Bennington Wentworth.

Governor Wentworth, in his wisdom, granted Moulton some land up in the Lakes Region and named it after his friend. He called it Moultonborough.

These were good old boys who were members of the club . . . the club being elitist and aristocratic.

And so it was that General Moulton bred a huge ox which he fattened to a weight of over 1,400 pounds.

And on a day in the fall of 1763, the general tied a huge British flag to the horns of the ox and, with fife and drums, marched from Hampton to Portsmouth. On the way, he attracted a great following for the parade, and hundreds of people arrived at the governor's mansion where the general presented his friend with the great ox.

Benning Wentworth was tickled pink.

What could he give his friend in return?

"Oh, nothing . . . nothing at all. This is all for the great esteem I feel for you."

"Oh, you must have something. I insist."

"Well . . . maybe. There is, up north near my grant in Moultonborough, a small gore of land I have rather liked for some time now."

"Then you shall have it! As a small token of my esteem for you."

And the governor then issued the grant to his modest friend.

That small gore of land . . . that small token . . . turned out to be some 27,000 acres which today comprise the towns of New Hampton (named for the general's hometown) and the town of Center Harbor.

Not a bad return . . . for a little ox kissing. ❧

Bears in Dublin

WOLVES, BEARS, WILDCATS, were all part of Colonial New England. All killed sheep and chickens and calves and pigs. The town histories are filled with stories of encounters with wild predators. And among these, the bears were the most feared because, unlike wolves and wildcats, bears were known to attack humans.

There are a couple stories in the *Dublin Town History* about encounters with bears. One concerns just downright-foolhardy courage or, maybe, anger, and the other concerns Yankee ingenuity.

In 1772, the history tells us, the wife of Ebenezer Cobb heard her pig squeal. The Cobbs lived just outside of town on lot eight. Mrs. Cobb—and the town history doesn't say what her first name was—grabbed her broom and ran to the pigpen. There she confronted a huge black bear holding her pig by the scruff of its neck.

She, that is, Mrs. Cobb, not the bear, was outraged and, hollering for help, she went right at the beast, slamming it over the head with the broom. The bear was confused and dropped the pig and ran away before any help came.

You'd think, after doing something like that, the town history would record her first name.

The second bear story concerns another Dublin resident, a guy named Aaron Marshall.

This was in 1781 and the Marshalls, too, were troubled by bears.

In this case they were trampling his cornfield. The old muzzle-loaders were not reliable in the wet. They misfired a lot so the prospect of facing a bear head on was a little more daunting then. So Aaron Marshall set a trap. He knew where the bears were entering his field. They had left a path there. Aaron Marshall went out and tied two guns to trees opposite each other. Then he ran a string from the triggers to cross the path.

Later that day he was at a husking at a neighbor's home when he heard the report of the two guns. He and his neighbors went out to see what had happened. Sure enough, a huge bear was dead.

The town history tells us that they then carried the bear back to Aaron's home and placed it on the floor in the living room. He awakened his son Benjamin, and put the small boy on the bear's back and everyone had a good laugh.

Apparently they couldn't find the Polaroid. But the story is almost as good.

And, of course, like you, I have speculated about what would have happened if the first to enter the field had not been a bear. ❧

Boys Chased by Wolves in Fitzwilliam

DR. SILAS CUMMINGS lived in Fitzwilliam back in the 1800s and he kept a diary. One of Dr. Cummings' stories is related in the *Fitzwilliam Town History*. It was written in 1877.

The doctor tells us that in the early days there were still wolf packs roaming the region. They killed sheep and pigs and chickens and, if the winter was particularly hard, they were reputed to attack people.

Now in the middle of the winter two little boys, one age seven and the other age nine, were sent by their father to drive a yoke of oxen from the extreme southern part of town to a house some miles away to borrow a cart and bring it back home.

The boys made the trek and got the cart and hitched the oxen to it and started for home but by that time it had gotten dark.

They had gotten three quarters of the way home when a pack of wolves appeared behind the cart, with the animals howling and barking and yelping in the darkness.

More than twenty years later, one of the boys told Dr. Cummings that his hair stood on end and his flesh crawled as he walked beside the oxen whipping them onward, while his brother cried as he sat in the wagon.

The oxen, he said, ran as fast as most horses. He, however, had no trouble keeping up with them, as his incentive was as strong as theirs.

There were, he said, mud holes and stumps and rocks and pole bridges to get over but, in the end, they arrived at their father's barn and went inside.

Although they heard the wolves, they never saw them.

Neither boy was harmed . . . at least physically. ❧

Shoes

EVER WONDER WHAT people wore for shoes or boots back in Colonial times?

I don't mean the rich. The rich had their shoes made by artisans or imported from England or the continent. But how about the dirt farmer in, say, Rye or Stratham or Epping?

These people had very little cash money. They were subsistence farmers. All they needed from the store were iron tools, pots and pans, needles, glass. Everything else they grew themselves . . . or made themselves.

But there were itinerant shoemakers. These guys traveled the countryside and lodged at the houses of the farmers with their shoe-making tools. Each farmer would supply his own leather from animals grown and slaughtered right there on the farm. The farmer also tanned his own hides although some towns had tanners.

Leather tanned on the farm was thick and long wearing.

According to the *Hampton Falls Town History,* each shoemaker would do a service called "whipping the cat." I don't know where the expression came from or why, but it meant staying with the family and working until he had created shoes for every member. After "whipping the cat" at one family, the itinerant shoemaker would then move on to the next family.

The shoes before 1805 were made much like moccasins. The shoes would be then covered with a legging called a "buskin." Buskins were hand knit from wool by the women of the house. Buskins covered the leg from the knee to the ankle and over the shoe itself. They were tied with leather thongs under the sole and up over the instep much as ski pants are held down nowadays.

In 1805, the first boots were introduced in New England. They were called "Suwarrows," named for a Russian general.

It was about this time that shoemaker and cobbler shops began appearing in the small towns. These operations made pegged shoes and very fancy boots.

Most farm people would go barefoot in the summer because shoes were so dear. Even in the winter the women, for instance, would walk to church with rags wrapped on their feet until they approached the meetinghouse. There they would don their shoes for the final walk into the sanctuary. ❧

First Workers' Strike

THE TOWN OF Sandown is the site of the first recorded workers' strike in America.

True story.

Seems back in 1773, townsfolk were building the fabulous Sandown Meetinghouse. In those days you had to have a supply of spirits on hand to keep the workers going, and this construction site was no exception . . . except that right after they got the framing up, it was discovered that the rum barrel was empty.

"Strike," said the builders. "We will go no further until we get what was promised us!"

"Oh, darn," said master builder Nathaniel Batchelder, who hitched up his team and started off at a trot for Newburyport, Massachusetts. There the rum arrived practically daily from the West Indies.

Batchelder returned the next day with a full barrel and a red face, and work recommenced. ❧

Nevins' Rock

ON THE COMMON in the town of Hollis is a stone taken from a road that once ran beside the Nevins' farm.

In Colonial times, farmers were required to build stone walls on either sides of roads that went through their property, and to maintain such roads. This labor was often done in lieu of taxes.

One day, three of the Nevins brothers, Benjamin, William and Phineas, were attempting to pull out this stone from the bed of the road beside their home. Using crowbars and chains, they had struggled all morning with the task.

Around two in the afternoon Deacon John Boynton rode up with news. "The regulars are killing our men," he said.

That day, by the way, was April 19, 1775, and Deacon Boynton was a member of the town's "Committee of Observation." The news he brought was about Lexington and Concord. It was the start of the American Revolution.

The brothers left off their labor. There, in the middle of the road, they wedged a smaller rock under the larger boulder so that they might continue the work when they returned.

They then rode off to Boston and Bunker Hill, and other places.

William Nevins was killed at Bunker Hill and a year later his brother Benjamin was killed in a battle in New York.

And the boulder in the middle of the road?

The boulder, with its smaller trig rock, was for seventy years left there in the middle of the road as a monument, a testament to the brothers who, without thought, left their home and labor to fight for their country.

When the boulder was finally removed from the road it was moved to the Town Common where it has been ever since. They call it Nevins' Rock. ❧

Nancy's Brook

HER NAME WAS "Nancy." We do not know her last name. Simply, "Nancy."

It was the year of the American Revolution, 1776, that Nancy came down from Lancaster to Jefferson to work as a domestic for Colonel Whipple and his family.

She lived with the Whipples two years and she fell in love with one of the Colonel's farmhands. He professed his enduring love and asked for her hand. She accepted.

The couple decided to marry in Portsmouth.

Nancy returned to her parents' home in Lancaster to prepare for the marriage. Before she left, she entrusted her two-years' wages to her husband-to-be. He wasted no time. The very next day he set out for Portsmouth. Without her.

Nancy got word that he had skidaddled. She, at once, started walking south, thinking that if she went on a run, she might catch up with him when he camped in Crawford Notch.

So off she went.

In Jefferson, at the Colonel's home, they noted that she was wet and very tired. They begged her not to continue. But she was adamant. And off she went into the freezing northwest wind. She traveled through the day and the night. In the Notch she did not find him, but she found the warm ashes of his campfire.

He was not far away.

She had taken nothing to eat with her, yet her passion drove her on.

Back in Jefferson they waited for her to return. Surely she would come to her senses. But Nancy did not come back.

A party of men set out to find her. They plodded through 22 miles of deep snow. In the Notch, they found the remains of the campfire. Beyond were the tracks of the lover and his friends and fresher tracks of a woman. Here the searchers rested for an hour, thinking that Nancy, too, had probably warmed herself by the fire. Then on they went.

A very short distance and they came to a brook. And there, sitting on a rock in the brook, was Nancy.

Her hand was on her walking stick. Her head rested on the hand and stick. Her dress and coat had been soaked through. Apparently she had fallen into the stream when she tried to cross.

She had frozen to death.

And her lover? Well, it is said that he heard the story and was conscience-stricken. They say he went mad. What is definitely known is that he died less than a year later in the hospital in Portsmouth.

And that is the end of the story, except that to this day, the hill above the brook where Nancy died is called "Nancy's Hill," and the brook is called, "Nancy's Brook." ✒

New Ipswich Mob

DURING THE AMERICAN REVOLUTION, feelings ran high against the British.

The people in New Ipswich heard there was a Tory sympathizer named Wilder down in Ashburnham, Massachusetts. So a posse of about fifty men was formed, and they took torches and went down to teach the man a lesson. Well, the mob got there and surrounded the man's house and three New Ipswich citizens, Josiah Brown, Isaac Howe, and Joseph Bates, were chosen to confront the man.

They scourged him out of his house and everyone jeered, and they required him to mount a barrel by stepping on the bung.

Mr. Wilder, the town history tells us, leaped atop the barrel, and the crowd was most upset. The men had him mount it again, this time using the bung.

If you don't have any idea what that means, you are not alone. I have no idea what it means, either. I guess it was some sort of humiliation. Anyhow, they made the man take some kind of oath, and everyone came back to New Ipswich, where the air was purer and there were no damned Tories.

Well, they may not have thought so, but the good people of Rindge had heard otherwise.

They heard that Judge Champney, who lived in New Ipswich, was indeed a Tory and that they, the good people of Rindge, had as much right to practice vengeance in New Ipswich as the New Ipswich mob had to avenge in Ashburnham.

So the Rindge patriots came marching over to tar and feather Judge Champney.

They were met on the road by the citizens of New Ipswich and were told to get the heck out of town; that the locals would take care of local matters themselves. And if they didn't leave, they would be set upon and beaten.

The town history tells us that the Rindge Patriots, seeing their errand superfluous, went home. ❧

Frenchmen's Duel

THE YEAR WAS 1782. This is a story that has been passed down as true, although the name of the local man is not known. It is worth telling though, because it is supposed to have happened in Portsmouth.

The French fleet was lying in harbor in Portsmouth. The town cemetery was then a field, and a man from Little Harbor was walking across on his way home. He looked out to see a rowboat from one of the French ships coming toward the shore down there.

Two of the men in the boat were officers. The other men pulled the boat up on the shore and the party came into the field.

The local man was about to leave when the group from the boat indicated that he should stay. They, of course, spoke French, which the man did not understand but their gestures were clear; they wished him to stay.

Immediately the two officers faced off and drew their swords.

It was a duel.

The men parried and lunged, and one of them was stabbed in the heart. The winner then presented the man from Little Harbor with a gold coin. They then loaded the corpse into the boat and rowed back to the ship.

Nothing was ever officially reported in Portsmouth. ❧

Shakers in New Ipswich

CULTS ARE NOT a new thing. In the 18th century, a strange dancing religion took the fancy of many people in New Ipswich and their behavior shocked the rest of the community.

The *New Ipswich Town History* has the story.

The history tells us, "It was one of the strangest delusions attended, with almost incredible extravagances."

The year was 1784. A number of people in the southern part of New Ipswich became aware of, and gave credence to, the divine mission of an English woman named Anna Lee. Her sect was called "The Shaking Quakers." We know them as the "Shakers."

The leader of the sect in New Ipswich was one Amos Whittemore. Mr. Whittemore held meetings of the group at his home on the south road at the foot of Whittemore Hill.

There, 40 or 50 people from New Ipswich and surrounding towns would assemble and practice their rituals. These rituals consisted of long and furious whirling dances. The New Ipswich history tells us that these performances exceeded anything in the annals of savage war dances. These rituals were attended with singing, shouting and shrieking which could be heard miles away from the Whittemore home.

The history says, "They resembled drunken bacchanals or raving wild beasts, rather than rational beings."

A stick was used to thump on the floor to keep time for the dancers. This stick was, for years, displayed at Captain Bailey's house in the village.

"Some of the practitioners," the town history says, "believed in witchcraft and their ability to perform miracles."

The rest of the town of New Ipswich was not sympathetic to the sect's cause and after a year or two, most of the members left town and joined others of their church in Harvard, Massachusetts. Among those who went was Amos Whittemore, who gave away his farm and possessions when he left with the other members of the faith.

Half-a-dozen years later, Amos Whittemore returned to New Ipswich where he moved in with, and was supported by, his son.

Whittemore's daughter, Sarah, claimed to possess supernatural powers. She, it was said, cast spells on cattle and other animals and things. Most did not believe it but, after her death, the local church denied her the common rites of burial and she was unceremoniously interred in a crude box of rough boards. ☙

The Cockade Hat

HOW A PERSON dresses is important. Shorts and a T-shirt aren't appropriate for a wedding and you don't wear a tuxedo to paint the kitchen.

Patriotism is also often judged by the way a person dresses. The Hippies and the Yippees and the Hells Angels are often viewed as subversive because of the way they use the American flag in their dress.

But political statements in the form of dress aren't a new thing.

Over two hundred years ago over in Milford, a doctor was trounced severely by townspeople for wearing a bunch of ribbons on his hat. The story comes from the old *Milford Town History*, and it is dated August 9, 1798.

Dr. John Peabody lived in what is now Mont Vernon. And one day he came down to Milford to do some shopping and to visit some friends. He arrived wearing a French cockade in his hat. A cockade, in case you don't know, is a bunch of ribbons . . . kind of a rosette.

Well, word spread that there was a guy in town wearing the colors of France. This was, of course, right after the Revolution and patriotism was rampant. So a mob went to the house where the doctor was visiting and told him to remove the French emblem.

He refused and further, he cursed the Constitution. He cursed it, he said, because it gave such riff-raff as this the kind of power they felt they had to tell a man how he could or could not dress.

Well, the mob went after him, and he went for a butcher knife. They took it away from him and, with it, cut up the cockade . . . and the hat. They then carried him into the yard with his feet in the air, made a circle around him and gave three cheers for Federalism.

The history then tells us that he was dismissed with the warning that if he showed up again with a French cockade hat that the Mill Pond would be at his service. ◈

Lightning

VIOLENT DEATH WAS common in early America. The town histories record that, by far, the most common unnatural deaths were by fires.

Drownings were also much more common years ago. The Jaffrey history records fourteen drownings over the years, including a horrible story of a one-year-old who fell into a vat of soft soap in her mother's kitchen.

There were also many suicides . . . mostly hangings.

But the surprise to me was finding out how many of our ancestors were struck by lightning. The *Jaffrey Town History* alone has half a dozen stories about lightning strikes.

The earliest record is for July of 1801, when eight-year-old Oliver Bacon was struck and killed at his home in Jaffrey.

In June of 1853, a yoke of oxen and five sheep were killed by lightning in Charlie Davidson's pasture.

That same day, over in East Jaffrey, Daniel French's house got hit and, next door, Joe Joslin's barn was also struck, leaving a mark on the outside but no persons or animals were injured.

In 1864, George Marshall, the 22-year-old son of Captain Abel Marshall, was killed by a lightning bolt in Jaffrey. The *New Hampshire Sentinel* reported that the bolt struck near the chimney which it shattered on one side, but that no marks were seen on the door where the young man had been standing. He had no marks on his body but, when people came to assist him, he breathed just once and died.

In August of 1870, a huge lightning strike hit a corn and pumpkin patch on the Charles Bacon farm and burnt a pattern of exploded pumpkins and seared corn 100 by 150 feet across. This time no one was hurt.

Obviously, the Bacon family was attracting some supernatural attention.

I say this because in August of 1872, lightning struck the barn of Oliver Bacon and killed a horse which belonged to a man named Luke Carter.

That strike also tore up the floors of the barn and, although Mr.

Bacon and Mr. Carter were both in the barn at the time, neither was hurt.

In 1810, Colonel Benjamin Prescott's home in Jaffrey was struck by lightning. Nine people were in the house at the time. One of his daughters was stunned by the bolt and fell to the ground. The lightning struck the chimney and tore off the ridge pole. Inside, it tore up a floor in one of the rooms, split a chest of drawers and smashed a bed as it zigged its way down to the cellar, where it tore a hole in the ground under a barrel where the Colonel himself was drawing a mug of hard cider.

No one was killed in the strike, but the Colonel's shoes were scorched.

It is not reported whether or not he ever got his cider. ✦

Surgery in Sharon

IN 1807, JOHN TAGGART, a man from what is now the town of Sharon, New Hampshire, was shot through the neck.

At that time, Sharon was a part of Temple.

It happened on October seventh. On that day the town militia was presenting a regimental review on the Temple Town Green.

One of the militia men was loading his pistol. The weapon was hot because it had been recently fired. As the soldier poured the powder and the wadding in, the gun went off. It was an accident.

John Taggart was standing beside the soldier. The wadding and powder from the gun tore through the back of Taggart's neck and blew a hole clear into his mouth.

Dr. Amos Twitchell from Marlboro was at the celebration and was, of course, immediately called. Dr. Twitchell noted that the wound was a black hole a good two or three inches in diameter. It was dirty and messy. Also John Taggart's jaw was smashed and the external carotid artery was torn apart. The carotid artery, in case you are wondering, is the main artery from the heart to the head.

The wound was, in other words, a mess. The patient should have been hemorrhaging. But there was very little blood. Dr. Twitchell dressed the wound and the patient was sent to his father's home in Sharon to await his death.

But John Taggart did not die. In fact, over the next week the wound cleaned itself.

On the eleventh day, as Dr. Twitchell redressed the wound and as he was leaving, the patient suddenly spewed blood out of his mouth. The carotid artery had opened and was hemorrhaging into the back of John Taggart's throat.

Dr. Twitchell, with the help of the patient's mother, managed to apply pressure to the artery. He then was able to tear the artery away from the muscle in the rear of John Taggart's throat and pinch it shut.

In the meantime, Mrs. Taggart got some thread around the artery and, following the doctor's instructions, tied it off with a surgeon's knot. But within ten minutes the wound was leaking again.

The doctor then packed sponges around the wound and held them in place with a bandage tied around the patient's head.

It worked. John Taggart recovered.

Later, Dr. Twitchell published a description of the operation in the *New England Journal of Medicine* and the article made history.

For this was the first ligature of the carotid ever to be performed by an American surgeon. ✎

Stool Pigeons

A STOOL PIGEON is someone who tells on someone else. But do you know where that phrase comes from? Do you know what a stool pigeon was originally?

Well, I found out what a stool pigeon is from a story in the *Bedford Town History.*

Seems that in the old times, before there was refrigeration, people preserved things by smoking them like ham or smoked salmon or cod . . . or they pickled them like corned beef or eggs or pigs feet.

And back then, the history tells us, there was a big market for pickled pigeons.

The country had millions of pigeons and there was an industry in shooting or netting these birds, eviscerating them and pickling them and selling them in cities like Boston.

One of the great migration routes of wild pigeons went directly over Bedford. In the spring, the birds would fly north to mate in northern Maine, and in the fall the birds would fly south again. At these times hundreds of hunters would try to trap the birds.

In Bedford, they would pick a field and scrape all the topsoil off a small area. Then they would scatter wheat and corn on the ground. Because there was no topsoil, the birds could see the bait from on high. Around this area the trappers would place a net with the edge held in bent willows or other spring poles. When the birds would fly down they would wait until a great number were there, and then spring the trap and the net would launch over the feeding flock and catch 'em all.

Now for the stool pigeon.

This was a live bird that was tethered to a stick in such a way that it would flutter in a circle.

From on high the flocks of birds would see the fluttering and swoop down to see what was happening. They'd see the corn and wheat and the whole flock would settle to feed.

Often they would catch three or four hundred birds at a time.

Often the birds were thin and the trappers would take them home and fatten them on corn for a couple weeks.

The birds were considered a delicacy and could bring as much as two dollars a dozen in the Boston market.

The town had half-a-dozen noted pigeoners over the years. The last man to make his living in such a way was Sam Morrison, who stopped the practice about 1870.

By then there were many fewer pigeons, and few flew over Bedford, as most farmers had ceased growing grains locally and there was no inducement for the birds to come this way. ✎

Londonderry Turnpike

WHAT A DIFFERENCE a road makes.

Think about it. When Interstate 93 went in, a lot of people who worked in Manchester and Concord and Nashua could, and did, move up north to live and commute from places like Ashland, Plymouth and Thornton.

That's what good roads do. They change the commerce and living patterns.

One of the first great commercial highways in New Hampshire took shape in 1804, when they began construction of the Londonderry Turnpike. The *Salem Town History* says the road was, "The most gigantic and important undertaking in road building that the town ever experienced."

The new highway ran in almost a straight line from Concord to the state line near Andover Bridge. How straight a line? Well, it followed what is now Route 28 and just look at that . . . the road, that is, the Londonderry Turnpike, was for its first 27 years, a toll road.

You paid to use it. And people used it like you wouldn't believe. Suddenly a farmer outside Concord could raise pigs or turkeys or sheep or cows and sell them in the Boston market.

The turnpike had walls and fences on both sides all the way from its start at Butter's Corner in Concord to the state line in Salem. Butter's Corner was located just across from the Route 3 bridge on South Main Street.

Even in the towns the highway went through, there were fences in the front yards of the homes to keep the driven animals on the highways. All up and down the road, there were fields and barns and taverns and inns where the drovers could pasture their animals and refresh themselves.

A lot of money was made over the years as the highway was one continuous conduit of animals and carts, even in winter, when sleighs plied the road.

The tolls varied. A penny for every ten sheep or ten pigs. A stagecoach or any vehicle with four wheels and four horses was four cents. It cost a penny to drive a yoke of oxen over the road.

The toll keepers were an independent lot, too. One keeper in Salem was a woman. Her name was Mary Campbell and, according to the town history, "She was a very tall, angular woman with muscles like a man, developed by the active life she led."

She kept a gun in her house with which she was proficient. She shot deer and turkeys and small game in the forest but, the history tells us, she also shared her board with a large cat who was a fine hunter, too.

He would bring home rabbits which he killed often, the history says, a considerable distance away. He would deliver them up to his mistress who would cook them and see that the cat also got a generous helping at meal time.

The highway remained a toll road until 1831 when the state took it over.

A dozen years later the railroad would come to New Hampshire, and the Old Turnpike would then give up its place as the premiere conduit for commerce in the state. ✍

Religious Revival 1814

SEPARATION OF CHURCH and state is again in the news with the attempt to take the phrase, "under God" from the Pledge of Allegiance.

But when it comes to government in America, religious controversy is not a new thing.

There was what was called "The Great Awakening" in 1740.

In 1810, a second religious revival swept America with a fervor that would be hard to match nowadays. This second revival lasted a dozen years.

Back then, of course, the townspeople were officially taxed to support a local church and its minister. It would not be until 1819 when the Religious Toleration Act was passed. But well up into the 19th century public taxation was used to teach what was called Protestant morality.

In 1814, the towns of New Ipswich, Mason, Rindge and Winchendon officially entered into a religious pact for, and this is a quote, "the better observance of the Sabbath."

In New Ipswich, nine tithing men were selected to make sure that no unnecessary labor was performed on Sunday, also that no traveling or other infractions of the day of rest were practiced.

The tithing men went so far as to stop and arrest strangers on the highway who were trying to travel through their town. The travelers were jailed until Monday morning when the sun rose.

Well, the tithing men soon found themselves in lawsuits and were obliged to abandon their police work.

And that was sort of the end of it.

But what I have always wondered was how the tithing men reconciled their police work of arresting people who weren't resting when they, themselves, weren't resting. ❧

Silver in Barrington

ONCE UPON A TIME, about 180 years ago, a wealthy widow lived with her son on a farm in Barrington.

The farm was known far and wide for its fertile soil. In fact, the place was called "Green Hill." The land was so rich there that, even in what was called "The Starving Year" of 1816, when all crops in New England failed, the corn grew at Green Hill.

In fact, this was the making of the family fortune.

Desperate people came to Barrington to purchase corn from Jeems Hayes, the man who owned Green Hill.

And Jeems, being a Yankee, scalped them good. Hungry people came and paid what Jeems asked, which was an entire silver dollar for each peck of green corn. And Jeems insisted that the coins be silver. He would have no other. At the end of the season, Jeems Hayes had become the richest man in town.

A couple years later, when the Strafford Bank suffered a panic, Jeems was able to bail the institution out with a loan . . . which made him even more rich.

He kept some money in the bank which he now controlled, but the silver coins that made his fortune in 1816 were kept in a trunk in his bedroom.

Jeems' son, James, was all the things his father was not. He was lazy and stupid, and he gambled and drank. When his father died young, James let the farm go to seed.

His mother was anything but pleased. And one night in early October, Young James and some of his cronies were playing cards and got very drunk in the widow's kitchen. There was talk of the silver coins in the trunk.

The widow panicked and went to the bedroom where she opened the trunk and scooped up the silver coins in her apron. She then went out to the barn where she found a spade and by the light of a half moon, she walked westward. She passed the old family burying ground and a way beyond she found a triangle of soft land with a large tree growing at each point of the triangle. It would be easy to locate again, she thought. And here she dug a hole and buried the silver coins.

A week later the Widow Hayes went back to locate the coins but she recognized nothing. She was lost.

So she went to neighbors and told them the story. Dozens of friends combed the area looking for three large trees around a triangle of soft land. But no one could find the place.

And that is the end of the story. To this day the silver coins have never been found. Or maybe someone did find them and never told anyone.

Whatever happened, there is still a chance that the coins are there in the soil, somewhere near Green Hill in Barrington, New Hampshire. ♠

The Tornado

IN 1955, A tornado tore through Worcester, Massachusetts, and up the center of New England.

I remember that day. I was nineteen and living in Milford. Trees were uprooted, barns blew down. It was a mess.

But that wasn't the most destructive tornado ever to hit the state. The most destructive tornado occurred in 1821, and there is a graphic description of it in the *Warner Town History*.

It happened on the ninth of September. Early in the afternoon, a huge funnel arose on Lake Champlain and moved due east across Vermont. It then veered slightly south, and went directly over Lake Sunapee, clipped New London, and plowed through Sutton. The great funnel came into Warner at the base of Mt. Kearsarge in an area called "The Gore." Here the wind exploded William Harwood's barn and tore the roof off Abner Watkins' house and blew his neighbor's barn to bits.

Seventy-two-year-old Samuel Savory lived with his son and his son's family in that part of town. The son was away for the day, but his entire family was there in the house.

They heard the thing coming. Samuel and the women went upstairs to close the windows.

They were too late. The wind lifted the entire house off its foundation and twirled it around in the air. When it came down it burst apart and buried six of the family members.

Samuel's wife suffered broken bones and many lacerations from falling timbers. Their son's daughter, Mary, had an infant in her arms when the wind hit. The baby was killed and the mother severely injured. Samuel himself was found dead a hundred feet away from the home on a stone wall, his skull crushed.

Half a mile away, John Palmer rushed to warn his family but was too late. He saw his home destroyed. His wife was badly hurt, but the rest of the family survived with minor scratches.

Fields of corn were swept clean. Trees uprooted. A stone weighing 600 pounds was carried several feet.

Anna Richardson was at the home of Peter Flanders and his wife when the tornado hit. He was killed and Mrs. Flander's baby was ripped from her arms. The child was severely injured but survived.

Over in Salisbury, all of Deacon Joseph True's buildings were destroyed; house, barn, sheds . . . everything. He himself was saved because a huge timber fell sideways and kept the falling walls away. The family had been baking bread, and the bricks of the oven were scalding hot. The Deacon dug his wife and four children out of the ruins and in doing so, burned the flesh from his hands handling the bricks.

All survived, although Mrs. True suffered many broken bones. Their youngest child, who was seven weeks old, was discovered a hundred feet away, protected by an upturned sleigh.

And we think things were dull back then. ✎

The Old Portsmouth Bridge

PHOTOGRAPH BY LAURA WALKER

BEFORE THE ROUTE I-95 bridge, before the Sarah Long Bridge . . . heck, even before the Memorial Bridge . . . if you wanted to go from Portsmouth to Kittery, you crossed the old railroad bridge.

Cars that didn't want to take the ferry used to rattle over the railroad ties when the trains weren't using the bridge.

The old railroad bridge stood near where the Sarah Long Bridge stands today. There has been a bridge in that location since 1822, and from the start it was controversial.

As you know, waterways were the highways of Colonial times in Seacoast towns like Portsmouth and Dover.

(Note the Wentworth Gardner Mansion and the Moffatt Ladd House. Both face the water because those coming to visit would, often as not, arrive by boat, and the mansions presented their faces to the docks just as landlocked homes faced the highways.)

So, if you wanted to go from Portsmouth to Exeter or Durham or Newmarket or Boston, you went the quickest way, by boat.

In the 18th and 19th centuries, Dover had a regular packet service to Boston. There were three ships so that one ship was in port at all times.

Goods in all the Seacoast towns arrived by ship.

The Great Bay trade was conducted with sailing barges unique to the area. They were called "gundalows." Over the years, thousands of gundalows carried goods all over the tidal estuary.

The reason I mention that is because, as the interior of New Hampshire was opened up, more and more roads were constructed. And roads meant bridges.

When the bridge between Portsmouth and Kittery was built in 1822, it created a hazard to navigation for the gundalows. Some of the fiercest tides found anywhere in the world are there in the Piscataqua River. The gundalows were always crashing into the bridge.

And, from the start, the bridge was a mishmash. It was a series of smaller bridges built on pilings driven into the mud of the river. Floods and ice and rot kept it in a state of constant disrepair.

By 1840 they started dumping huge stones into the river for a more permanent base for the pilings. That, of course, created more treacherous currents for the gundalows, and the selectmen of Dover sued the bridge people for creating a hazard to navigation.

But the damage had been done. The stones were already in the river.

And then the railroads came. The bridge was reinforced even more and the gundalow accidents increased tenfold.

Insult and injury. The railroads took away most of the commerce from the gundalows. The railroads could carry coal and bricks and all sorts of goods that used to come by water, and do it cheaper.

And, on top of that, they put this barrier in the river that smashed the gundalows.

Today there are no gundalows from that time left. There is, however, a beautiful and historically accurate re-creation of a gundalow. It can be seen at the docks opposite Strawbery Banke in Prescott Park in Portsmouth.

But the old railroad bridge went the way of all old things. And what replaced it?

Well, in case you haven't noticed, the lower section of the Sarah Long Bridge is a railroad bridge. I haven't seen a train go across it in years though. ✍

The Funeral Ride

BENJAMIN EASTON WAS dead. He died of a heart attack in Sullivan, New Hampshire, on February 21, 1822. He was sixty years old.

The funeral was held at his home in Sullivan, and half the town turned out for it. That was because Ben Easton had been a popular man . . . and also because it was known that Ben's wife was a good cook and there would be lots of good food and rum.

So a lot of people turned out. And the corpse was laid out in the spare room, as was the tradition in New England funerals in the early 19th century, and the minister said his words and there was some praying. And then, as was the tradition, the folks repaired to the kitchen for some food.

Too many, it turned out.

The Keene Sentinel reported, "Just as the services were concluded and the people began to move, the floor in the kitchen gave way and the spectators were precipitated into the cellar."

The floor, it seems, went down quite slowly and only one person suffered any broken bones . . . an older lady who broke two ribs. A couple other people suffered bruises but, on the whole, it was just a ride down.

People whooped when the floor went down and the deceased's grandmother screamed, "Save my soap!"

Soap was homemade back then, and very valuable. ❧

Shot by His Own Gun

IT HAPPENED OVER 260 years ago in Fitzwilliam.

It was mid-August, and Major D.T. Hayden was coming home from a day of hunting, when he paused to observe some of his neighbors who were improving the roadway.

Mr. Hayden was a popular and highly regarded man who, among other things, was a member of the Fitzwilliam Fire Company.

As he watched the men work, the major leaned on his musket. It was a mistake, for while doing so, the firearm discharged. Major Hayden fell dead on the spot.

Now the reason we know all this is not because it is in the history (although it is), and not because it is part of the local folklore; rather, the reason we know about the incident and exactly where it happened is because of a 15-foot-high obelisk that was placed near the spot where he died by his friends and family, so that he would not be forgotten.

On a slate tablet affixed to the stone is this inscription:

"To the memory of Major D. T. Hayden who fell and died upon this spot by the accidental discharge of his own rifle August 18 A.D. 1838, age 30."

The major himself is buried in town. ·✸

The Hat

IT IS JUST as true nowadays as it ever was. If you are carrying a large roll of bills, it is best not to flash it around strangers.

The *Nelson Town History* had this story about a man who was imprudent about flashing his cash and came close to having it stolen. What saved him was his hat. The story took place in the mid-19th century.

The man's name was Oliver Stone, like, but no relation to, the movie producer, and he was a cattle drover. A number of times a year he would drive cattle from Nelson to Boston, where he would be paid a great deal of money for the bunch.

On the way back from one of these drives, he stopped at a tavern for supper, and when he paid for the meal didn't bother to hide his wad of cash.

He then left the inn and found that it was raining. He mounted the horse and unrolled the brim of his hat, which he usually kept rolled back from his face. He then rode off.

A short distance down the road, two men stepped from the woods and grabbed the horse's reins and demanded, "Your money or your life!"

The first man then raised a lantern and looked at Mr. Stone and exclaimed, "This ain't the man!" and dropped the reins.

In that instant Mr. Stone saw his chance and took it. He spurred the horse and outran the robbers.

Later, back home in Nelson, he told friends that the hat had saved his life. ✎

Our Nig

HERE'S SOMETHING THAT is worth knowing. The first novel in this country by an African-American was written by a woman from Milford.

Her name was Harriet E. Wilson and she was raised as an indentured slave at the home of a man named Samuel Boles and his family.

The book is entitled, *Our Nig, or Sketches from the Life of a Free Black, in a Two-story White House, North, Showing That Slavery's Shadows Fall Even There.*

The book was published the summer of 1859, just before the start of the Civil War.

The book is said to be a "roman à clef," which is to say, a true autobiography of Mrs. Wilson, although all the names in the novel have been changed including the author's name. In the story the protagonist is called Alfredo or simply, "Fredo."

It is a challenging story to read—both in the fact that the style is of the time, that is slightly florid and obtuse; but, more than that, this is a story of child abuse and bigotry that matches that of *Uncle Tom's Cabin.*

I don't mean to say that you will not like this book. I, in fact, read it at a single sitting. I could not put it down.

In this narrative, "Fredo" is the child of a white woman who, earlier, has had an illegitimate child that soon dies. Filled with shame, she is forced into extreme poverty. Here she is befriended by a black man who marries her and Fredo is born. The black husband gets sick and dies and Fredo is abandoned at the home of a local family. Her mother goes away never to be heard of again.

Fredo's mother knows the mother of the family she has left her with is a martinet and meanspirited but feels she has no choice.

The rest of the novel is about pettiness and beatings, unfairness and hopelessness.

It shows Milford to be a place where no one will save poor Fredo, but rather turn their eyes away from the injustice they see. The title of the book sums up the patronizing and rudeness of its citizens.

This is surprising to me because, of all the towns in America, Milford developed a reputation as a center of the abolishionist movement. William Lloyd Garrison spoke from the stage of the Milford Town Hall. As did Frederick Douglass.

In 1851, the citizens of Milford raised a subscription of money to purchase the freedom of a runaway slave who was being tracked by bounty hunters and was hidden in the home of Zenophon Mills on Clinton Street.

The world-famous Hutchinson Family Singers of Milford were the foremost champions of abolition in America.

Milford was a major stop on the underground railroad.

Still, Harriet Wilson's book rings true to many and I, for one, would like to see her book read more widely.

And the author, herself, deserves notice for her contribution to this very American art form, the personal novel.

There is an organization called "The Harriet Wilson Project," dedicated to getting the Wilson book read in the schools and also the creation of a memorial to her name here in New Hampshire. ❧

The Witch of Coos

ONE OF THE scariest stories around is Robert Frost's poem, "The Witch of Coos."

It is the tale of a French-Canadian mother and son named LaJolie who live on a small farm up "north of the notches." The mother freely admits to Frost that she is a witch.

As the evening progresses they tell of some bones that assembled themselves and walked up from the cellar one night and ended up in the attic of the house.

The woman had had her husband, Theophile, nail the attic door shut. Then the couple pushed their bed against the door to keep the apparition locked away.

That had been years ago. Theophile now was dead.

That night the woman decided to tell Frost the truth. And that truth was that the bones had been those of the woman's lover. Theophile had killed him and then he and his wife had buried the dead man in the cellar.

Great stuff, this poem. It might be fiction, or maybe not.

But the truth be known, there really had been a witch in Coos County. Not the one Frost wrote of, but another that did horrible things as well.

The story is in the *Stark Town History*. And everything I am about to tell you is true . . .

It all happened during the Civil War, about 1864.

Joe Leighton had gone out to his barn one morning to find something horrible. He called his wife and children and they could only stare with open-mouthed astonishment. Joe's two oxen were dead in their stalls. But what was chilling was the way they died. The animals had been hitched together into just one bow of a yoke. Both animals had strangled.

Within a week another neighbor had gone out to find his oxen in the same way, strangled to death in one side of a yoke.

Over the next few years other farmers around Stark found their pigs and sheep and calves also strangled.

Joe Leighton came home one day to find his bull with its tongue cut out.

There was, most agreed, a witch somewhere close by. Joe Leighton went into the house and melted down a silver plate. From this he molded a silver bullet with which he shot the bull. He hoped, by doing this, he had also killed the witch.

But the witch did not die. Later that week the Leightons discovered that the inner works of their clock were missing. The works were made of wood. Later Joe found the works on a beam way up in his barn.

He took the works back to the house and left them on the table. The family then went to bed. In the morning he found the clock reassembled and ticking on the mantle piece.

A week later Joe came home one evening to find the roof of a shed had blown off. But there had been no wind that day. No one knew what had happened.

People in Stark felt the Leightons were cursed.

Joe's wife, Hattie, kept her Sunday clothes in a locked trunk and kept the key to the trunk around her neck at all times. One Sunday she unlocked the trunk to find her clothes torn and dirty and covered with swill.

All these things happened within a ten-year period. And then they stopped.

People in Stark felt the witch had probably died. Or gone away.

But it would be forty more years before the witch would actually die.

The witch's name was Abigail Walker and she lived then in West Milan.

Abigail Walker was on her death bed when she called her friend, Ida Wentworth. She had to get something off her conscience . . . something that had burdened her her entire life. She did not wish to meet her maker with the secret unconfessed. Here's the story she told:

Forty years before, she and her brother Jim had done all the horrible things that the people of Stark had suffered those ten years.

As you have probably figured out, Ida was the daughter of Joe and Hattie Leighton.

It all started when she and Jim had been playing in the barn when they wondered if they could get both oxen into just one side of the yoke. They had succeeded but were unable to get the thing off.

The next day they were horrified to find that the poor animals had panicked and had suffocated. The fact that their father and his friends had, right off, suspected witches had been an convenient way to get off the hook.

To keep the suspicion going, the two had killed animals at other farms in the area.

Also it was fun. They were at the center of the commotion. Everyone talked about it.

But to keep the adults blind to their sin they had had to do more and more vicious things. The worst had been cutting the tongue out of the poor bull.

The clock they had both disassembled and reassembled.

As to the clothes, their mother had fallen asleep early one evening and they had taken her key from around her neck. Then they went to the pigpen where the hogs had ruined the garments. Then they returned the key to the sleeping woman and no one was the wiser.

As to the roof coming off the shed. There had been a keg of black gunpowder in the shed and the kids had taken handfuls of the powder to the fireplace where they threw it in and watched the fireworks. After half a dozen trips between the shed and the house they had dribbled a trail of powder which, at one point, caught fire and backtracked itself 'til it reached the keg. And, *Kaboom!* The roof blew off.

Joe and Hattie Leighton had gone to their graves thinking all their woes were witchcraft. Abigail, however, died with a clear conscience.

And that's the story of the real "Witch of Coos." ✎

Ben Thompson and UNH

THE UNIVERSITY OF NEW HAMPSHIRE might never have been located in Durham had not an old skinflint farmer named Benjamin Thompson been a total klutz at romance.

Here's the story:

Seems Benjamin Thompson was a very bright guy. He believed in science. And in the middle of the 1800s, he set about using scientific methods in the running of his farm. He succeeded in a spectacular way, especially in the growing of fruit. Ben created hybrids and grafts and special fertilizers and reaped huge harvests of apples and pears and peaches on his farm. He was soon the richest farmer in the county.

But Benjamin Thompson, fine as his methods of agriculture were, was not a social man. In fact, he had few friends. He tended to give in to his temper and was often petulant. His help stayed with him because he was such a good farmer and because he paid them well. But he was not well liked.

He was also . . . how do I say this? . . . He was, well, not good looking. So his appeal to the fairer sex was less than limited.

At one time he fell in love with a young woman from Portsmouth and he visited her and her parents and told of his prospects and his successes and asked for her hand. She turned him down. She had accepted a proposal in marriage from another just days before. Ben was heartbroken and went back to his farm where he made the land produce as it never had before.

Ten years went by and Ben again fell in love, this time with a young woman in Concord. And this time he was in possession of a fortune. He was, from a material point of view, a catch.

But this time the young boys in Durham heard that old Ben was "goin' a courtin'" and they waylaid him on the highway with ribaldry and jest and startled his horse and destroyed his self-confidence.

Ben never got to Concord, and the young woman often wondered why he had not returned. But, in some way, she felt relief. For there were family pressures for her to accept him. And now she didn't have to.

And so it went until 1850 when Ben turned 44 years old. That year, he learned that the woman he first had courted in Portsmouth many years before had become a widow. This brightened his prospects considerably. A widow with four children couldn't possibly turn him down. And so she did not.

Ben refurbished the old farmhouse in Durham. Added a porch and had the parlor fancied up.

He then gave his bride-to-be $1,000 to purchase furniture and rugs for the house. She was delighted and went to Boston where she purchased the fanciest stuff available (see, back then a thousand bucks could buy a lot).

Well, the furniture came and the bride-to-be was there in the parlor moving it around when Ben came in from the fields ugly as a goose and cussed as a mule. He took one look at the new furniture and declared it, "Ugly." He kicked a chair across the room and declared it, "As impractical and uncomfortable-looking as any pile of sticks I ever saw."

And so it was, the bride-to-be became the bride-not-to-be. She quietly left and, to the day he died, there was never a mistress in Ben Thompson's home.

But the farm continued to prosper and, in the end, there were no heirs to leave it to, and so Ben gave it to the state to be an agricultural school.

And so it was that the University of New Hampshire would owe its location in Durham to a man with a cussed personality . . . and a broken heart. ☙

Josiah Pike Hanged

THOMAS AND ELIZABETH BROWN, an elderly couple, were living on a farm in Hampton Falls in May of 1868.

That evening as she was preparing dinner, Elizabeth heard a knock at the back door. When she opened it, she was confronted with a man wielding an ax. The man swung it down upon her head and she fell. The man then entered the living room where Elizabeth's husband was sitting by the fire reading the newspaper. Again the ax fell.

The next morning, the hired man arrived to find the couple unconscious and lying in pools of their own blood. Miraculously, they were not dead.

The doctors were summoned. Mrs. Brown was deemed hopeless and she died within hours, never regaining consciousness. Thomas Brown, however, regained consciousness within a day and was able to tell authorities who it was that had felled him.

The assailant was, Thomas said, one John Ross, a man who for some months had been working there on the farm. Only a couple days before he had quit his job. To go west, he had told them.

John Ross was, most everyone said, a great guy. He was personable and pious, smart and hardworking. He was also handsome.

The authorities went looking for him. Within a day he was discovered in Newburyport . . . and with his arrest, came a surprise.

Seems he was not John Ross, after all. That was an alias. His real name was Josiah Pike, and he was a member of a respected family in Newburyport.

He was, however, the black sheep of the family. He was, it turned out, a thief and a drunkard and a dissolute person.

Six days after the arrest of Josiah Pike, his second victim, Thomas Brown, also died.

Pike was jailed in Exeter and bound over for trial in October. There he was found guilty.

The motive for the crime was money. Thomas Brown had recently sold a brace of oxen for some hundreds of dollars. Pike had seen that Mr. Brown kept his finances in his desk and had rifled the desk, but had not found the money other than eight dollars of household cash.

He had also missed a sum of money kept in the desk for the local church, of which Mr. Brown was treasurer.

The court found Josiah Pike guilty of murder and ordered him hanged.

This was after the Civil War, and recent law required that a man be kept a year in the state's prison before sentence was carried out.

During that time the newspapers had a field day and, because he was handsome and witty and had found religion, many young ladies in the Concord area visited the condemned man. He had high celebrity. In fact, a ladies choral group would visit Josiah Pike and serenade him in his cell.

Pike's relatives, being wealthy, hired the best attorneys and made every effort to have his sentence commuted from hanging to life imprisonment.

Their efforts did not work. In November 1869, Josiah Pike was hanged inside the state's prison in Concord. It was the first in-camera hanging to be carried out. Before that, executions had been open to the general public.

An hour before Josiah Pike's death, a contingent of women visited him bearing many bouquets of flowers. They then sang to him . . . and went away weeping. ☙

First Cars

THE FIRST AUTOMOBILE ever built in America was built in Sunapee, New Hampshire, by Enos Clough in 1869. The story is provable, and why it is not a part of general history is not known.

The first rubber tire automobile in New Hampshire was built by a father-and-son team from Manchester in 1896. It was a two-cylinder, steam-powered runabout, made by Peter Harris and his son Leander, who lived on Amherst Street.

They made the car from scratch out of bicycle wheels and wood and other parts that were at hand. The machine developed 260 pounds of steam and burned soft coal or wood, and could travel non-stop from downtown Manchester to the Halfway House in Hooksett, a distance of about seven miles.

The contraption was steered by a tiller which moved the entire front axle much like a child's wagon. It went about as fast as a man could walk.

Leander, himself, designed and built the engine from scratch. In the winter, and other times when it was not being driven, the automobile was displayed in the front window of the William Farmer Shoe Shop on Elm Street and was a great curiosity.

The machine was used for about three years. We don't know where it is today.

Manchester Alderman Albert Clough bought the first gasoline-powered machine in New Hampshire, a two-cylinder St. Louis, which he drove himself. He became such an expert that for years he wrote a thrice-weekly newspaper column entitled, "Hints for Motorists." Dozens of papers around the country carried his advice.

The first four-cylinder automobile in New Hampshire was owned by Governor Charles Floyd of Manchester. Governor Floyd did not drive it, but his chauffeur, Oscar Bemis, did. It was a Thomas Flier, a very fancy machine. This, of course, was back when only the very rich could own automobiles.

Even then, they were dirty and loud and scared the horses. Passengers had to cover themselves with dusters and goggles as they were out in the open and there were no windshields. ✎

The Great Souhegan Bank Heist

ON THE EVENING of the 19th of October, 1874, Frederick T. Sawyer heard a knock on the front door at his home on Souhegan Street in Milford.

As he opened the door he was confronted with a revolver pointed straight at his head.

Six men rushed into his home and quickly found Sawyer's wife, Sarah, and their children: 14-year-old Bertha, 12-year-old Frederick, and 6-year-old Chester.

All were gathered into the living room, bound and gagged, and stuffed into closets. The men then found an auger and bored holes in the doors of the closets so that the hostages would not suffocate.

The men were there because Sawyer was the cashier of the Souhegan Bank and he had the keys to the vault. They waited until after nine o'clock.

They then hustled the bound-and-gagged victim across the rickety footbridge over the Souhegan River, onto Nashua Street, and to the bank, where they looted over $100,000 in cash and bank bonds. This amount in today's money would be over $25,000,000. It was, in fact, about the entire worth of the town. Milford faced total bankruptcy.

Although Frederick T. Sawyer escaped with his life and his family was unharmed, none of the cash was ever recovered.

Later it was learned that the robbery was the work of known bank robber George White. He was assisted by two burglars from England, another unidentified man, and another bank robber from New York City named Tom McCormick.

All this is known because the mastermind behind the crime was another bank robber who called himself Max Shinburn and who, at the time of the robbery, was on the lam living in England.

Later Shinburn spent time in the New Hampshire State Prison. In 1913, he answered a letter from Sawyer's grandson Donald, asking if he knew who pulled off the Souhegan Bank job. He did know. They were friends of his.

You may wonder how the town overcame such a heavy loss.

Well, catastrophe was averted by the bank's president, William A.

Towne. Towne contacted the Boston underworld and let it be known that he would buy back the stolen bonds. Most of the businesses in town had put their money in these bonds and President Towne felt responsible.

He ended up paying a dime on the dollar. He ransomed the bonds back for $20,000 and thus saved most Milford businesses from bankruptcy.

But many had lost confidence in the bank and pulled their money out. Also, Mr. Towne was criticized from the pulpit and around town for compromising with criminals. As a result he took his own life. ❧

Train and Shotgun

BACK IN 1891, there were a couple of truly unfortunate occurrences in the neighborhood of the old Number Eight Schoolhouse just north of Jaffrey.

The first happened in July, when Miss Florence Taft was driving her carriage and horse with her passenger, Mrs. Asabel Raymond.

As they came across the tracks near what is now Hadley's Crossing, the pay train on the Fitchburg Railroad came barreling down and hit the rig and carried the horse and passengers some 125 feet down the tracks where they were deposited in the river.

Mrs. Raymond was thrown from the carriage and suffered minor scrapes and bruises, but Miss Taft and her horse were instantly killed.

Miss Taft, the history tells us, came from Greenville and was a clerk in George Duncan's Drug Store. It also says, "She was a most attractive lady."

That was in July.

Two months later, when school was open at the old Cheshire one-room schoolhouse, the kids were horsing around before school and were plugging green apples at each other. At the same time, there was a horse and wagon there in front of the school.

Well, one of the apples went astray and hit the horse between the eyes. The horse, in turn, reared up and kicked the wagon and a shotgun that was on the seat of the wagon fell into the back and went off.

The shot tore into one little girl's abdomen, and some of it hit another in the lip and broke her tooth . . . a third girl was hit in the leg.

All recovered, but the teacher had a little talk with the kids about plugging apples. ✒

Goose Yokes

ACCORDING TO Cornelius Weygandt in his book *The Heart of New Hampshire*, people used to yoke geese like oxen and make them pull carts.

Mr. Weygandt notes that he himself owned two of these yokes and that they were very like regular oxen yokes. They were whittled from white pine, two inches by two inches by fifteen inches, with seven inches between the two yoke parts where the goose's head was inserted.

Weygandt's neighbor, Harry Blanchard, personally remembered a pair of geese in Meredith Center that had been tamed to pull a child's cart. Harry said that the geese were controlled with a modified ox language.

Oxen, he said, are smart and know a lot of commands besides *gee* and *haw*, and it was the same with the geese. They, too, were smart and knew their names and were very controllable.

The practice of yoking geese apparently went out of favor in the latter part of the 19th century, about the time that the practice of harnessing dogs to dogcarts went out of favor.

Dogcarts came back about the turn of the century, but no one has seen a trotting brace of geese pulling a cart in a hundred years.

I don't know about you, but I see an opportunity here. ✎

Snow Rollers

Snow roller, Department of Transportation, Concord.

UNTIL THE LATE 1920s or early '30s, if you had an automobile, you put it up on blocks from the first snowstorm until the mud season was over in May.

No one plowed the roads back then.

In the winter, you used horse and sleigh or oxen or railroad, or you walked.

Oh, there were some hearty folks who took the wheels off the front of their Model A Fords and put skis on the front and a kind of bulldozer track on the rear. These kits were the first snowmobiles in America and they were made right in New Hampshire . . . up in Ossipee.

But, for the most part, people used sleighs. And, frankly, a sleigh could transport much heavier loads than wagons could in the summer. Most logging was accomplished in the winter, for instance.

The first snowplows came to the state about 1929.

Before that they rolled the roads.

See, after each major snowfall, towns in the Granite State would take out these huge wooden rollers, and with really large teams of horses or oxen, they would pack the snow down so people could get around driving sleds and sleighs and pungs.

A big snowstorm meant extra money for a lot of people. Teenagers could get a dollar a day shoveling snow off or on a road helping the rolling operation. A buck a day back then was what a grown man made.

The teams that pulled the rollers were made up of Morgan and other horses owned by the farmers in the community. After the storm, they would join their teams together to make teams of six or eight or even ten horses that were required to pull these huge contraptions.

Some towns preferred horses . . . other towns, oxen. Often it was dictated by what was available.

It was a happy time for those who did the job. It meant companionship; working with your friends . . . not to mention the extra money. Even the horses seemed to enjoy the change of work.

The shovelers knew where the snow would pile up because of the wind.

Year after year, it was always in the same places.

Other places the wind blew the snow away and these places needed snow shoveled on them. The inside of covered bridges had to be covered with shoveled snow so the sleighs could easily skid through.

But all this changed when the first plows arrived. By the mid-thirties, the snow rollers were no longer used. And the thousands of rollers in the state were, literally, put out to pasture. According to historian Charles Robinson, in the early 1950s, there were more than a dozen rollers just rotting in the fields in the towns around Conway alone.

The last testament of an era gone by. ☙

The Lancaster Fox

IT'S BIG ENOUGH to be a wolf. But it isn't a wolf. It is, clearly, a fox. But a fox much larger than any fox ever was.

There is a monument to, as the tablet on the monument tells us, "the brave men and women who redeemed Lancaster from the wilderness." It was presented to the town of Lancaster by the Unity Club back in 1913 on the occasion of the 100th anniversary of the founding of the town.

But why, you may ask, a fox?

Ah, well, yes, there is a story here.

It's a story that starts with a service organization founded by and for the women in Lancaster back in 1904. They called themselves the Unity Club and their first project was to plan the first Old Home Day ever for Lancaster. That happened in 1905 and it was a huge success. So much so that, they not only paid all the bills, they actually made a profit of $20.

The ladies voted to put the money toward a monument. The monument would be a simple granite boulder with a plaque. It would be unveiled on the 150th anniversary celebration of the town in 1913.

Over the next eight years the club raised quite a bit more money toward the monument. It would be placed at the front of centennial park and unveiled by a direct descendant of the original founders.

Turns out one of the original founders of Lancaster was Lt. Emmons Stockwell. Lt. Stockwell's grandson was a wealthy businessman living in Washington, D.C., Emmons Stockwell Smith. It was Mr. Smith who provided the extra cash so that the monument would not be a simple granite boulder, but rather a granite boulder with a fine piece of statuary on it.

Now I know, we still haven't explained why a fox . . . and, more importantly, why a giant fox. Well, bear with me.

See this time, that is, the turn of the century, was a time of powerful families, and powerful families controlled everything and they had their favorites. This was the time of Henry Adams and the sculptor Augustus St. Gaudens and architects H.H. Richardson and Stanford White and landscape designer Frederick Law Olmstead. These were the people who dictated taste.

If you were on their "in" list you were a success.

Well, the creator of this fox was a member of the aristocracy. She was a talented sculptor and daughter of a famed paleontologist. Her name was Anna Vaughn Hyatt, and she sculpted, almost exclusively, animals . . . horses, dogs, lions. She did a grand statue of Joan of Arc . . . on a horse, of course.

Anyhow, the sculptor was on the "A" list and was commissioned by the Frederick Law Olmstead Firm in Brookline, Massachusetts, to create an animal fountain for one of their park designs.

No one seems to know why, but the sculpture was not, in the end, what the Olmstead firm had in mind. And so there it was.

Enter Emmons Stockwell Smith, who knew the sculptor and the work and could afford to purchase it . . . not for himself, mind you, but as a grand gift to the town of Lancaster. What better? The fox is native to the hills around the town. Perfect.

Of course, young Emmons Stockwell Smith Jr., would unveil the work and little Ruth Stockwell Gardner would scatter water lilies in the basin of the fountain on that grand day . . . as they did.

And all was a grand success. Well, not really. A lot of people scratched their heads that day. "Why a fox?" they wondered.

And, to this day, they still wonder, "Why a fox?"

The answer is, of course, "Because it was available." Pure and simple. ❧

Breaker Breaker

BACK IN AUGUST of 1979, a guy on a CB radio up in New Hampshire's White Mountains saved a ship off the coast of South America and, to this day, no one seems to know just how it happened.

George Quig was the man's name, and on the tenth of August he was up in the White Mountain area, when he tried to call his wife on his CB radio. He didn't get her but he did get an SOS from a ship at sea.

George Quig thought it was a hoax. The SOS came in clear as a bell in an area where he had trouble contacting his wife just a few miles away. The voice calling the SOS said the ship was off the coast of Venezuela.

Of course it was a hoax. Had to be a hoax.

But the caller seemed earnest, so George Quig found a telephone and called the Coast Guard and they, in turn, called South America, just in case.

Turned out there was a ship in distress and, due to George Quig, three hours later, five people were rescued from a 42-foot trawler off the coast of Venezuela, just where they were supposed to be.

But nobody seems to know how a radio signal from two thousand miles away was received on a simple CB radio up in New Hampshire's White Mountains.

The best explanation is that it was an atmospheric quirk, an oddity in the ozone somewhere that bounced the signal up and down and up and down to finally settle in a pinpoint place where George Quig just happened to be.

But, frankly, that's just a guess. ❧

Sauce for the Goose

BACK IN 1988, when I was living on Nubanusit Lake over in Hancock, we had a scandalous romance that had everybody talking.

He, the suitor, was handsome and arrogant . . . and she, the suitee, was a wild thing who had come down from Canada to spend the summer with her lover. Every day they would cruise around the lake stopping at every beach and every floating raft, where he would strut around and intimidate the property owners while she remained on the water.

Now, I must tell you, this is not exactly what you might be thinking.

He was a domestic white gander from a farm down at the end of the lake; and she, a wild Canada goose.

We on the lake were crazy for the idea of the two of them being in love . . . that is in the abstract. Problem was, the gander, in protecting his sweetheart, would attack anyone on their beach with a vengeance. He ran me off my own beach a number of times. It was scary.

I would back away from him using a lawn chair like a lion tamer.

Also, the goose was nasty and we could no longer walk barefooted on the lawn which was a mottled surface of dead grass where . . . well, suffice it to say, the lawn never looked better . . . the next year.

But that year . . . oh, I would have dreams of that goose. And in my dreams she always appeared with orange sauce.

The romance continued all summer, although at all the meetings of the lake association the couple was denounced.

In the fall, I'm told, the goose went south. And the gander, I'm told, went in the oven.

I have no idea if there were any orphaned goslings.

Fact is, I don't even know if that could happen. Do you? ✺

THE TOWNS

How Towns Got Their Names

MOST TOWNS IN New Hampshire were named after other places:

Manchester, Portsmouth and Canterbury are all in England.

Some towns, like Derry and Antrim, were named for places in Northern Ireland.

Laconia is a German place.

Goshen and Canaan are biblical.

Many towns were named for people:

Jaffrey, for Lord Jaffrey.

Walpole, for Sir Robert Walpole.

Fremont for the "Free Soil" candidate, John C. Fremont.

Washington, New Hampshire, for the guy with wooden teeth.

There are Native American names too: Nashua and Contoocook and Merrimack.

And there are places in New Hampshire that came by their names in a more romantic way.

Before the area was incorporated, it was called the "North Woods" by the lumbermen who cut and dragged the trees from the forests down to the Great Bay. The first permanent settlers came in 1763, and the town incorporated ten years later. And kept the name.

It is Northwood.

Back in 1756, the area was settled by the Robinson, Smith, Shepard and Batchelder families. Most of those families are still around. Back then, there were thousands of deer in this area of the state. The story is that in 1765, when the families were negotiating for a town charter, two men of the town killed a fourteen-point buck and took it to Portsmouth, and presented it to the Colonial governor, Benning Wentworth.

Governor Wentworth was delighted and, in recognition of the gift, gave this place its name. Yes, it is Deerfield.

And Lempster.

Lempster was named after the Massachusetts town of Leominster. The problem was that back in the 1700s, everyone pronounced Leominster, "Lempster," and there was no official spelling for anything. So, to this day, it's "Lempster." ☙

Ashland

THERE WAS AT one time a pretty substantial potash business in the town of Ashland, but it was not this that gave the town its name.

Originally, the town was a part of the town of Holderness. Holderness was chartered first in 1751. At first, the proposed center of the town was on the high ground of the area in a section called Church Hill.

New Hampshire, like all the rest of America, was agricultural back then and the high meadow was where the meetinghouses were built. But when the West opened up, agriculture became less important in New England and manufacturing became the way most people made their living.

In this town the first mill was established down by the river. By the Civil War, that is where many of the people in town lived. They called the area the Flat Iron or Holderness Village.

Well, as the years passed, the Village became the place where the *hoi polloi* lived . . . that is the poorer quarter. At town meeting, the land owners and others saw to it that the Village got very little improvement . . . no public water or sewer.

So the inevitable happened.

In 1868, the Village petitioned the Legislature to become its own place, separate and apart from Holderness.

Now, an aside here.

Back in the 1850s, a young man from Holderness went to live in Washington, D.C., and became an assistant sergeant at arms in the Congress. While there he met and became an ardent supporter of Senator Henry Clay. The young man was Colonel Thomas P. Cheney, and when he returned to Holderness, he was one of those who petitioned to have a new town made of the old village.

Now one of the names proposed for the town was Oakland, because of the number of oak trees in the area. But Colonel Cheney proposed they name the town after the home of his hero, Henry Clay. He proposed the name Ashland.

Clay was well regarded in the Granite State.

And, so, Ashland became, Ashland. ❧

Fort Atkinson

IN THE FALL of 1746, a bunch of militiamen out of Portsmouth arrived at Little Bay on the shore of Winnisquam Lake in what is now the town of Sanbornton.

There they built a substantial garrison and named it after their commander, Colonel Theodore Atkinson.

Fort Atkinson was tight and warm, and the men stayed the winter—fishing, hunting, and drinking, and generally having a great time.

The fort was built under orders from Colonial Governor Benning Wentworth. The governor needed a northern picket post; that is, a place to serve as an early warning against the incursions of the French and Indians . . . a place to slow them down should their attack come through this region.

But that winter there was no such incursion.

The troops at the fort, the Carroll County history tells us, spent a year in idleness under the lax discipline of the provincial commanders.

When summertime came, the troops went on expeditions and camping trips all around the area. They had a great time, kinda like the Boy Scouts on camporee. They climbed the mountains and walked all around Lake Winnipesaukee, which back then was called Winnipiseogee, and they ranged as far north as the Sandwich Notch.

They kept diaries, made maps, and returned to Portsmouth with great stories and wonderful descriptions of the lakes and forests in the region.

Back home people thought the expedition a failure, a romp as it were, in the woods.

But the expedition was not a failure.

Fort Atkinson continued to provide protection and shelter to travelers in the region. And the glowing reports of the area, along with the terrific maps, made people want to visit the region as soon as possible.

And so when the French and Indian War came to a close in 1760, there was a veritable land rush in the Winnipesaukee basin . . . a rush that continues to this day. ✒

Webster in Boscawen

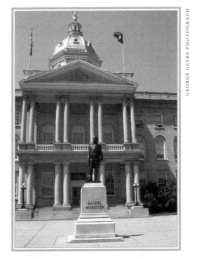

GEORGE GEERS PHOTOGRAPH

Daniel Webster Statue, Statehouse

THERE IS A rock with a plaque on it in Boscawen. Did you know that Daniel Webster had his first law offices there? The plaque shows where the offices used to be. That was, of course, a long time ago. 1805 to be precise.

Daniel Webster was born just north of there in what used to be Salisbury.

I say "used to be," because after Daniel got famous the town of Franklin moved its boundaries just enough so it incorporated the birthplace within its town limits . . . stole the area, as it were, from Salisbury.

They could do this because Franklin then had the mills and a lot of money and political power, and poor Salisbury stayed small and powerless. So the big guy took over the little guy's major asset.

And henceforth, people boasted that Daniel Webster was born in Franklin. He wasn't. And I, for one, think Franklin should give it back.

But when Daniel moved off the homestead, he moved there.

Another thing, did you know that Daniel Webster had a brother who was also a lawyer? Well, he did. His name was Ezekiel Webster and for a while he also lived in Boscawen.

Before he lived in Boscawen, Daniel had a lot of debt owed to his alma mater, Dartmouth. At that time he was not yet a lawyer, he was, rather, teaching school and, along with paying off his student loan, he was also sending money to Boston where Ezekiel had enrolled in college.

But Daniel himself needed to get to Boston in order to study law. So, along with paying Dartmouth and his brother's tuition, he also was saving up to purchase his fare to Boston . . . and he was doing this all on a school teacher's salary.

But luck interfered. Someone in Boscawen gave Daniel Webster a horse as a present. Daniel rode the horse to Boston. When he got to Boston, he gave Ezekiel the money he had been saving up for coach fare before he got the horse. That went a long way toward paying Ezekiel's tuition. And Daniel sold the horse and was able to pay Ezekiel's board bill.

The result was that Ezekiel graduated and got a job as a clerk in a law office and was able to support Daniel while he read for the law. Scratch my back.

Apparently Ezekiel was as brilliant as his brother, but is little noted in history other than as the brother of Daniel.

Daniel also practiced law in Salisbury and, of course, in Portsmouth, before going to Massachusetts to become famous. ✿

Center Harbor Named

ONE OF THE proprietors of the town of Londonderry back in 1719 was a young man named John Senter.

John's son, Joseph, was captured by the Indians during the French and Indian War. This son was taken to Canada to be ransomed back to the Colonies. But Joseph was clever and watchful and managed to escape his captors.

Later, Joseph Senter and his brother, Stephen, were settlers in the Lakes Region. They ended up as proprietors of a hotel on Lake Winnipesaukee.

In the early days, the land was a part of New Hampton, but in 1797, the citizens, including Joe and Steve Senter, petitioned the legislature to incorporate their own town.

The suggested name was Watertown, as there was a deep harbor on the lake. But Watertown could apply to any town on the lake just as well.

As the town was equal distance away from Meredith Harbor and Moultonborough Harbor, and, as one of the most-noted families in the area was the Senter family, it was decided to incorporate under the name of Center Harbor.

Now they didn't spell it Senter Harbor, but they didn't spell it Center Harbor, either. They spelled it Centre Harbor . . . that is the English spelling. Very tony. But the Senter family knew that the homonym was a tribute to them as well as a description of the location of the town.

Later they went over to the present spelling of Center Harbor. And that is what it has been called ever since.

I guess they decided against Senter Harbor, because they knew nobody would ever spell it that way. ❧

Charmingfare

TALK ABOUT POETIC names.

The settlement was originally called "Charmingfare."

It was called "Charmingfare" because the people who settled it thought it was so pretty. But then when the citizens petitioned the Colonial governor to become a town, Governor Benning Wentworth exercised his prerogative as the ultimate authority of what places in New Hampshire would be called. He named the place after the capital of Crete.

Y'see, after his graduation from Harvard, Benning Wentworth sailed to Europe on one of his family's ships. He visited the Greek island of Crete and thought its capital, Candia, charming... and fair.

So in 1763, Charmingfare, New Hampshire, became Candia, New Hampshire. And Candia it has remained ever since.

Ninety-six years later, in 1859, Candia's most famous citizen was born. He was christened Samuel Walter Foss.

Sam Foss grew up to be a poet... well, he wrote verse. My mother used to quote Sam Walter Foss all the time. She loved his work. So did my Aunt Harriet. Mother loved Eugene Field's poems, too, and Aunt Harriet loved Edgar Guest's poems.

This is something that people don't do much anymore. Used to be, at family reunions, people would recite. Kinda like the karaoke of its time. It was something that was done to show off and entertain. This was back before TV. In Mother's and Aunt Harriet's case, it was back before radio even. If you had company back then, someone would play the piano and the kids would recite... and so did the grown-ups.

At Christmas Mother would do, "Father calls me William."

Aunt Harriet would do:

> Somebody said that it couldn't be done
> But he, with a chuckle replied,
> That maybe it couldn't but he would be one
> Who wouldn't say so 'til he tried.

Or she'd do "The Cremation of Sam McGee" or "Casey at the Bat."

But, by far, the most recited piece of verse of the time was written by this man, born in Candia, Sam—and by the way, he insisted on Sam, not his birth name, Samuel—Sam Walter Foss.

I think you can guess what the poem is, but before I tell you, let me tell you a couple things about Sam Walter Foss.

He was the class poet at Brown University, which he graduated from in 1882. After graduation he worked in New York and Boston as a newspaper reporter. He was, for many years, the editor of *The Boston Globe*. He founded the Candia Club, which held literary meetings and presented noted writers of the time. The Candia Club meetings were held in his hometown, and also in Boston. The club was known nationwide. He was also the librarian of the Somerville, Massachusetts, Library and he was a founder of the Fitts Museum, as fine a small-town museum as exists anywhere and the first of its kind in New Hampshire.

So you see, the guy was something.

And his most famous poem?

His most famous poem was based on part of Homer's *Iliad*:

> *Fast by the highway an ever-opened door*
> *Obliged the wealthy, relieved the poor.*

Or, as Sam Walter Foss put it:

> *Let me live in my house by the side of the road*
> *Where the race of men go by;*
> *They are good; they are bad; they are weak; they are strong;*
> *Wise, foolish . . . so am I.*
> *Then why should I sit in the scorner's seat*
> *Or hurl the cynic's ban?*
> *Let me live in my house by the side of the road*
> *And be a friend to man.*

And, by the way, Sam Foss's house by the side of the road still exists in Candia. ❧

The Chester Cemetery

"Smiling Angel"

IN CHESTER, NEW HAMPSHIRE, is one of the few cemeteries in America listed on the National Historic Register, and it is worth a look around.

The cemetery dates from 1732, when one Sampson Underhill was buried there. His gravestone is not to be seen nowadays, and it's thought that he is somewhere under a road leading through the yard. Tread softly, for it appears there may be half a dozen or more unmarked graves there.

There is also a single grave with two persons buried in it. Major Jabez French and his wife, Hannah, were married in 1743, stayed together 63 years, and died within four days of each other.

Not all the stones there may be taken for granite, there's also a gravestone made of tin. You have to rap on them to tell.

And there is the epitaph for Lydia Webster, "All is Light Now."

But I think the most interesting stones are those carved by the brothers Webster—Stephen and Abel. Those carved by Abel smile, and those carved by Stephen, frown.

The story for this seems to be that Stephen became born again. He joined a Pentecostal group, which tried to convince the Congregational congregation to convert. They refused, and Stephen went off to Hollis, which had a church more to his liking. People liked his work though, and continued to use him, but from that time on he carved only frowning angels.

The cemetery houses Revolutionary War soldiers, scientists, pioneers, educators, men and women of letters. Back in the 19th century one of the town fathers, Nathan Morse, was quoted as saying, "Chester is like a hill of potatoes . . . the best part is underground." ⋄

Concord's Bridges

The I-93 bridge can be seen in the background.

WHEN NEW HAMPSHIRE was first settled, the mode of transportation was usually water. The first towns were on the Piscataqua River and Great Bay and later up the Merrimack and the Connecticut. As long as the ice was out, goods could be moved easily by water.

But soon land away from the sea and the rivers became places where people settled. And so there came a need to connect these inland places with those places of water.

In 1796, the state's first turnpike was built from the Piscataqua Bridge on Great Bay to a point in East Concord on the banks of the Merrimack River. The road was 36 miles long and was called, aptly, the "First New Hampshire Turnpike."

Where the road ended, there was a ferry across the river. It was called Eastman's Ferry in honor of Captain Ebeneezer Eastman, who had headed a committee to build the ferry some 70 years earlier.

There were two other ferries also operating in Concord . . . Kimball's Ferry just downstream . . . and Tucker's Ferry just a little way upstream. Tucker's was the newest, created in 1785.

Right after the turnpike was completed, the first bridge across the

Merrimack was built at the site of the Tucker Ferry. It was wooden and lasted five years before a freshet took it out.

Over the next 75 years, some five different bridges would be built across the Merrimack and each one would succumb to the floods. Five more wooden bridges were built over the Merrimack in different places in Concord between then and 1915. Each succumbed to flood or wind.

Wooden-bridge building was an ongoing occupation in the 18th and 19th centuries in New Hampshire. Throughout history, 11 wooden bridges were built across the Merrimack River in Concord alone. ✎

Dover

THE NATIVE AMERICANS called this place "Newich wan nock," which meant "Place of Wigwams."

In 1623, two brothers from England, William and Edward Hilton, settled at a place on the Piscataqua and called it after themselves, Hilton's Point.

Further up the river the Indians called it "Cocheco."

Ten years later, the upper town was being called "Bristol," after the English town where the newer settlers had come from.

A little later on, the local minister, Thomas Larkham, began calling the place after his home in England. He called it "Northam."

But in 1641, this place was finally incorporated as the town of "Dover."

It may have been named for the city in England, but historians feel that the name came, not from the English place, but rather from one Robert Dover.

Robert Dover was an English soldier who created the "Cotswold Games" as a protest against the emerging Puritanism of the time. These games were referred to as "Mr. Robert Dover's Olimpick Games" in the Cotswolds of England. The games included sports such as wrestling, running, jumping, handball, rural dances, and shin kicking. Dover didn't like Puritans at all. And apparently neither did the citizens of the town.

And so it has been Dover ever since. That is, except for a time just after the Revolution, when there were plans to change the name to Franklin City after Benjamin Franklin. Somehow the War of 1812 put an end to these plans.

New Hampshire's first historian (and some say finest) was Jeremy Belknap, a Congregational minister who lived there in the 1700s. A lot of people wonder why they never considered naming the town after him.

There is no town of Belknap but, of course, there is a county named after him . . . Belknap County. ♠

The Greenfield Fair

IN THE TOWN of Greenfield, where the Hancock Road and the Peterborough Road come together—right across from the entrance to Greenfield State Park—there is a ball field and open area that, at one time, was one of the most noted places in the entire state.

At one time, special trains were chartered from Boston and Lowell and Nashua to go there. Thousands of people arrived there every year to attend one of the most popular events in the whole of New England . . . the Oak Park Fair.

My uncles, Ned and Glen, and my father used to tell me about the fair. There was nothing like it, they said. It was the most fun of the whole year. It was not a goody-two-shoes fair. There were, in fact, things that went on that you kept the kids away from. There were girlie shows and gambling and horse races and fights. Everything a young man of the time hoped for.

The fair started as an idea some locals had back in 1875, just a few years after the Civil War. A bunch of boosters from the surrounding towns put up some money to construct the fairgrounds. They built a race track and a big exhibition hall with dozens of stalls for livestock.

That year the fair was a giant success and made the backers a ton of money. But subsequent years were iffy. Sometimes they made money; sometimes they lost money. In 1885, the corporation went belly-up. Within half a dozen years the buildings had all been torn down. But the half-mile racetrack remained.

Then, in 1899, some new people got together and raised a lot of money to rebuild the buildings and reintroduce the fair. They also built a huge grandstand overlooking the racetrack with a gigantic stage facing across the field. Along with a new exhibition hall, there was a baseball field and a new bandstand.

The draw was sulky racing, but there were also acrobat and vaudeville shows and a carnival and midway with sideshows and games of chance . . . and, of course, hoochie-koochie dancers.

The farm boys and men brought their prize animals and poultry.

The women brought their best sewing and cooking just as they do at county fairs to this day.

In 1915, the fair was renamed "The Hillsborough County Fair," and the event continued for another ten years.

But, as happened before, the fair gradually lost favor with the public; 1925 was the last year it was held. As the years passed, the trees gradually took over and, by the mid-1960s, it was a small woodlot. Little remained of what was once there.

Today the field has been partially reclaimed with a ball field. You can still see the outline of racetrack if you look for it.

It is also a great place for metal detectors. Lots of 1905 pennies have been found there. ☙

The Brickyards

IF YOU STAND on the West Side and look across the river at Manchester, you will be looking at a great deal of material that once belonged to Hooksett.

And that is because most of the bricks you see in the Amoskeag Mills came from Hooksett.

For a hundred years or so, Hooksett was famous for its brickyards.

That is because there is some wonderful clay right beside the river in Hooksett and, before the railroad, most goods were transported by barge and riverboat. It was a perfect combination. The clay was mined and mixed on-site and fired and loaded aboard a river barge and transported down river (another advantage) to Nashua or Lowell or Boston.

Later, of course, the railroad was built beside the river which gave the advantage of sending the bricks north as well.

By the time of the Civil War, there were five different brickyards operating in the town. Each one turned out five- to seven-million bricks a year. Twenty-five railroad flatcars a day took bricks all over the country.

The biggest yard was owned by Nat Head and his brother, William. The brothers were grandsons of Colonel James Head, who was a hero and fought with John Stark at the Battle of Bennington. Nat became governor of New Hampshire in 1828.

The Head brickyards closed during The Great Depression and today, other than old photographs, there is not a reminder of the industry that once controlled this town. ☙

Amoskeag Mills

FROM THE BEGINNING, the mills defined Manchester.

As a matter of fact, the name Manchester was chosen because, in the early 19th century, Manchester, England, was the largest producer of cloth in the world.

In 1805, Benjamin Pritchard built a small cotton and woolen mill at the Amoskeag Falls. The town was then called Derryfield. Five years later the townspeople renamed the place Manchester.

What ego, what gall, what an embarrassment! We have a rustic town of a thousand people aspiring to the title of a great English city.

The mill grew and expanded and, 23 years later, it was purchased by a group of Boston entrepreneurs; a group of men so powerful they ended up owning the water rights to the entire Merrimack River, Lowell, Lawrence, Manchester. They called their new operation after the falls, The Amoskeag Cotton and Woolen Manufacturing Company; and the mill grew a hundred times. The period, between 1838 and the start of the Civil War, was called the Utopian Period. The money poured in.

During this time the owners of Amoskeag took care of everything. Manchester became a planned community. The mill provided housing for the workers and gave loans for them to purchase it. There were clubs and sports teams and schools and banks and paid-and-planned vacations . . . cradle-to-grave security. The workers gave their lives to the mill, and the mill took care of them. It was supposed to last forever. It did not.

With the Civil War came more demand for cloth, but after the war there was a glut of fabric. Amoskeag could no longer be benevolent. And the workers unionized. The Utopian Period was over.

However, through good times and bad, the mill continued to grow and, by the turn of the 20th century, old Benjamin Pritchard's prediction had come true: Manchester, New Hampshire, was turning out more cloth than Manchester, England. Amoskeag was the largest textile mill in the world.

Seventeen thousand workers poured into the mill every day. The

Amoskeag Mill took up an entire mile on both sides of the Merrimack River. The operation covered eight million square feet; larger, in fact, than the World Trade Center would be, or the Pentagon.

And the place was totally self-sufficient. Raw cotton and wool came in one end and out the other end came cloth. Every operation was done on-site. The mill had its own carding and spinning operations, its own dye plant, its own looms. The washing operation even used soap from its own soap-making factory.

Amoskeag had its own machine foundry which also turned out steam engines. And because it made steam engines, it broadened out and also made steam fire engines and railroad locomotives. At its height, it was turning out one locomotive every week.

Later it made its own electricity from the water power.

If you lived in Manchester between 1840 and 1940 and you didn't work at Amoskeag, chances are some member of your family did. Manchester was Amoskeag, and Amoskeag was Manchester.

Until the 1930s, no other kind of business could settle in Manchester without the permission of the mill owners.

But things got nasty by the 1920s. Styles had changed, and the fabric turned out by the mill was no longer in demand. And factories in the South had newer machinery. Labor was cheaper in the South. The raw produce, that is, cotton, was closer by. In 1922, the workweek was increased from 48 to 54 hours and wages were cut by a fifth.

Workers struck, and the mills closed for nine months. There was a second strike in 1933, the middle of the Depression. This time there was bloodshed and sabotage. Two years later Amoskeag went belly up. It was all over.

From 1838 to 1933—the mills lasted just five years short of a hundred years.

The Depression was bad all over America, but no place suffered more than Manchester. It took until World War II before anything like prosperity came again to the Elm City.

Local Manchester businessmen took over the mill buildings and tried to attract new businesses there. Some businesses did use the buildings but most remained empty. In the 1960s and '70s most of the Amoskeag Mills were torn down. The paving stones were torn up and the canal filled in. Today you'd hardly know they were ever there.

Manchester is no longer a mill city.

Manchester is now a high tech city.

And 1936 is a long time ago, but there are still those who worked there who personally remember Amoskeag. And they all have stories. ✒

Marlow

LAURA WALKER PHOTOGRAPH

IT IS MY humble opinion that there is not a town in the State of New Hampshire that is more perfectly laid out or in a more perfect setting than the town of Marlow.

It reflects its image from across the pond in thousands of calendars.

You want a perfect picture? Come to Marlow.

Now there is a reason why this town looks so perfect, and that reason is because all the buildings that you can see were placed in relation to one another at one time, just as you might arrange some miniature Christmas village on your mantle.

The fact is, the town of Marlow used to be somewhere else, up on Marlow Hill to be exact.

When the town was chartered, Marlow, like other towns, put its center in the center of its area; equidistant to all four corners and on an upland meadow. That way people could walk to town meeting or church and back home while the sun was still shining. And the trip home would be downhill.

But then the Industrial Revolution came along, and towns that used to have mostly farmers now had more people working in the mills. It was the same in Marlow. By the second half of the 19th century, most of the townspeople lived near the factories by the water-power and on the flats where the railroads were built.

So the town, in its wisdom, voted to move all the public buildings from the high meadow down closer, and they had the luxury of saying, "The church goes here and the Grange hall there."

Which is why Marlow is so pretty. ☙

Lake Massasecum Named

THIS STORY COMES from the *American Guide Series, New Hampshire*, published in 1938, by the federal Works Progress Administration.

Back before the American Revolution, there was a hunter by the name of Eastman who set out to explore the Contoocook River Valley. One day he climbed Mt. Kearsarge and saw, in the distance, a column of smoke coming up from beside a lake. Mr. Eastman went to investigate.

There, beside the lake, he found an older Native American at his campfire. The man was alone.

It turned out the old Indian spoke some English, and he and Mr. Eastman sat by the fire and had a meal. Later the man told his story.

Seems he had been a powerful sachem, an Abenaki, back when the area was first being settled. The Indian attacks, he noted, had resulted only in heartbreaking reprisals and massacres of his people. As a result he urged his tribe to sue for peace. But because of his counsel, the tribe banished him, his wife and infant son.

He came there, he said, close to a white settlement. But the settlers treated him with suspicion. He was not welcome. His baby died, he said, and soon after his wife also died. He showed Mr. Eastman their graves.

Now, he said, he was alone, unwanted by his tribe and rejected by the white settlers.

Mr. Eastman, however, was fascinated. He spent many weeks in the company of this Native American. But winter came on, and he left to return to his home on the Seacoast.

The next year he returned to his friend's camp and found the old Indian dead. He buried him beside his wife and child.

Oh . . . and the Indian was named Massasecum.

And the lake that was named for him is Massasecum Lake in Bradford. ☙

Middleton Town Hall

MIDDLETON CORNERS, NEW Hampshire, population 1,400, isn't on the road to anywhere.

To get to Middleton Corners you have to be going to Middleton Corners. And once you get here you may think to yourself, as I did, "Why would anyone want to come here?"

Middleton Corners, as its name suggests, is a crossroads. The main street starts in Farmington and ends in Wolfeboro. The other road goes from New Durham to Union.

A new town-office building occupies one corner of the crossroads. Across the street sits a town hall which is as nondescript as the fire station that sits beside it. Not promising if you are looking for history, which is why the treasure you will find in Middleton is so delicious!

For there, in the upstairs of the town hall is this: a complete Meetinghouse, totally intact.

The boxed pews in the room are just as they were when they were built in 1795, and then there is the mural . . . a primitive mural of trees, painted in 1804 by an itinerant artist named John Avery.

Not much is known about Avery except that he painted the scene when the Meetinghouse was located in a different part of town. Oxen moved it to its present location in 1812.

At the same time, they built a new hall underneath the old Meetinghouse and turned the building from one to two stories. The downstairs incorporated a secular space with a stage and a small room to serve as a library.

The religion preached there was Free Will Baptist.

And a note here: the first Free Will Baptist Church in the world was built just next door in New Durham by the Reverend Benjamin Randall in 1780. The faith was practiced there until a new church was built in town in 1959.

The town hall is still used for town meetings and one religious service is held each August during Middleton's Old Home Day.

You can make arrangements to see the hall by calling the Middleton Selectmen's Office. The people in this town, it turns out, are like their mural—that is, very nice. ✎

New Boston's Eagle

SOMETIME, BACK IN the mid-1800s when New Boston's old Meetinghouse still stood, the town fathers decided that a cupola would add some grandeur to their town, and so one was added.

Half a dozen years later, the town fathers again decided that the town needed a bit more prestige and they proposed that a gilt eagle be carved and placed atop the cupola.

Subsequently they sent to Massachusetts to get an estimate of the cost of such a decoration. It would be expensive, it turned out.

Well, the town had lots of debts and was not rich and feelings ran high about the eagle. The supporters felt art above all. The non-supporters said, "Phooey, not with my tax dollars!"

Nevertheless, the article for such a gilded eagle was on the warrant come Town Meeting Day.

The selectmen spoke to the matter and were about to carry the day when one Joseph Dunbar, a local farmer, stood up and spoke his mind in such a way that the exact speech has been preserved to this day.

"Gentleman and others," he said, "I always reckoned the voters of New Boston were big fools and probably always would be. But, if they are willing to give five honest-to-goodness gold eagles for one gilt one, they are a darn site bigger fools than I had supposed." And he sat down.

No eagle ever adorned the old New Boston Meetinghouse. ❧

Newbury Gets Its Name

IN 1750, King George II of England returned to his homeland for a visit, his homeland being Germany. I know, that is complicated; but, yes, the English had a German King. George II also ruled over Hanover, in Germany.

Anyhow, this trip by the English king back to his homeland was reported in the news and celebrated all over the British Empire, including America. It was motherhood, the flag, and apple strudel.

One of the people most enthusiastic about the king's visit was New Hampshire's own Colonial governor, Benning Wentworth, who resided in Portsmouth. See, in his youth, the governor himself had spent time in Germany. He loved the place.

So, to commemorate his sovereign's visit, our good governor named three places in his colony after places in Germany. In 1753, he named one place "Dantzic," for the Baltic seaport. The town just north of it he called "Heidelberg." And over on the Connecticut River he picked out a town and named it "Dresden."

However, a year later, the governor had second thoughts about his names. A bunch of his cronies from Harvard College decided they would like that land, and the governor made them all grantees. At the same time, renamed "Dantzic."

He called it "Hereford" where, they tell me, hurricanes seldom happen. The new name was in honor of Edward Devereaux, Viscount Hereford.

Well, 18 years went by and the Harvard buddies of old Benning failed to fulfill the terms of the grant. So the new governor, John Wentworth, got new grantees and again, renamed this place. Now it was called "Fisherfield," after Governor Wentworth's brother-in-law, Captain John Fisher of the Royal Navy in Portsmouth.

"Fisherfield" lasted 60 years. But then in 1837, the town incorporated. By that time, of course, we were a state and the governor then was Isaac Hill. At the time, there were a lot of families who had settled there from Newbury, Massachusetts, and they petitioned to call the place after their old town.

And so, from that day, and maybe forevermore, this town has been called Newbury.

Oh, and the other towns?

Well, the town to the north, once called "Heidelberg" is now New London. And the place on the Connecticut called "Dresden" changed its name but not its nationality. It is now Hanover. ❧

Maxfield Parrish Stage

The Maxfield Parrish set survives in Plainfield

AUTHOR J.D. SALINGER lives somewhere near Plainfield, although the natives won't tell you where.

A hundred years ago, the area was crawling with painters and sculptors and architects. They were known as the Cornish Colony or, as the locals called it, "Little New York." Their center was down the road at the summer home of sculptor Augustus St. Gaudens.

By mid-century, most of the artists of the Cornish group had died off, save for one, the great American artist Maxfield Parrish. He is known for his posters, and he lived in Plainfield. He continued to paint right up to his death in 1966.

Now the reason I bring this up is because in the middle of Plainfield there is a piece of Parrish art that is unique in America . . . in fact, unique in the world. It is a stage set, a backdrop for theatricals. You'll find it in the old town house.

Stage settings are, by their nature, temporary things. They are built for productions and after the production is over they are "struck" (theater talk for "taken down"). After the play, the set is painted over and used in another production. Or burned.

As a result, almost no theatrical settings survive; only photographs of the settings remain.

But this set survives. And it appears to be the only set designed by a major artist to have survived anywhere in America. It survives because over the last eighty-odd years, no one seems to have come up with a theatrical production to replace it.

Parrish designed this work for a town stage show back in 1916. Local theatricals were all the rage then. Locals did skits and sang songs and recited. It was all good fun. The setting is local. It shows Mt. Ascutney and a body of water that appears to be the Connecticut River.

This piece of Americana has been conserved through the efforts of the Plainfield Historical Society. There is a new lighting board that shows off the painting in a way that makes most people catch their breath.

Is it worth a visit? You bet! ❧

Richard Nixon Profile

BACK IN 1941, one of the most destructive forest fires the State of New Hampshire ever suffered roared up from Stoddard, over Pitcher Mountain, and down into the Marlow Valley, burning nearly everything in its path.

The fact that the town of Marlow itself was spared was due to the industry of the local people who hosed down the buildings in the center of town. That, and a change of wind, was all that saved those lovely old halls and churches.

After the fire was doused, people out on Route 123 looked up and saw something they had never seen before, something the trees had always hidden from view: a profile of a man carved in the rocks up there. It was the first time anyone had ever seen the Marlow Profile.

The profile, unlike the Old Man of the Mountain, is bas-relief. It also is not rugged, as the Old Man was. Rather it has a silly, ski-jump nose . . . like Bob Hope . . . or Richard Nixon. And, in fact, many people call this the Richard Nixon Profile.

And, yeah, it does look something like Dick Nixon.

'Course, what do I know? My favorite anthropomorphic wonder is Monkey Rock over in New Boston. ❧

Oyster River Plantation

UNTIL 1732, THE town of Durham was a part of Dover. It was called "The Oyster River Plantation."

Most places founded by England in those days were called "plantations." Think of Plymouth Plantation and Jamestown Plantation. Dover itself was called Piscataqua Plantation.

Hey, the English even called Ireland a plantation.

Anyhow, this was Oyster River Plantation, beside the Oyster River.

Oyster River Plantation's first minister was the Reverend Hugh Adams. He was a Harvard graduate and an admirer of England's first Puritan bishop, one Richard Barnes, Bishop of Durham.

You got it.

It was the Reverend Adams who petitioned the Colonial governor to make the place of his congregation a town, and he suggested the name. He also said that he intended to govern the town in the way the English bishop had governed his diocese.

In the early days of the town, there were many Indian attacks and massacres in the area. In fact, the town maintained fourteen garrisons in various places within its boundaries.

One of the great Revolutionary War heroes lived there. General John Sullivan's homestead still exists there on a hill just up from the Oyster River.

One of the earliest settlers in Durham was Ebenezer Thompson whose great-grandson, Benjamin Thompson, left the family farm to the State of New Hampshire in 1890. Old Ben specified that the land was to be the location for an agricultural college.

That farm is today the University of New Hampshire. ✺

Pawtuckaway Boulder Field

THE BOULDER FIELD at Pawtuckaway State Park was discovered because people went looking for it.

Seems that in 1878 New Hampshire Governor Benjamin F. Prescott was upset because no boulders had been found in this state to equal those found in the adjoining states. So he sent out a searching party and they found some.

The erratic rocks lie in the half-mile-long notch between the north and south peaks of the Pawtuckaway Mountains.

The first one you come upon is Chase Rock. It is 40 feet long, 40 feet wide and 30 feet high.

The next is Churchill Rock. Churchill Rock is 60 by 40 by 40 and is said to be named for a lunatic (that's the word used in the history) who escaped his keepers and got atop this rock and couldn't get down. They say he climbed up the crevice in the rock but couldn't climb down the crevice. To get him down they had to fell a tree over onto the rock. Churchill was then able to climb down the tree.

Further down are more rocks and other debris in an area about 50 feet wide and a 100 feet long.

Here you will find four other rocks, the largest of which is Ballard Rock. ◆

Peterborough Library

THE FIRST FREE public library in the world supported by taxation is in Peterborough.

And yes, I did say, "in the world."

But a more important phrase here is the phrase, "supported by taxation."

Now there had been lots of free public libraries around supported by universities and churches and private benefactors. There were even subscription-supported libraries open to the general public. But the Peterborough Library is the first in the world where people got together and voted to be taxed for its support.

Here's the story:

The minister at the Unitarian Society down in Wilton was a man named Abial Abbott. While he was there, he founded a social library. Social libraries were all the rage back then—"back then" being around the turn of the 18th century. Small private groups would incorporate and purchase books in a time when they were expensive and nowhere near as common as they are today.

Peterborough, too, had established its own social library in 1790. But the books wore out and the library was abandoned.

But then, Dr. Abbott was reassigned from Wilton to the Peterborough Unitarian Church. There in 1828, he established what was called a "juvenile library," a library that students and the general public could use. He kept the books in the parsonage parlor. It was a great success.

About that time, Dr. Abbott helped form "The Peterborough Library Company," which was a private-subscription library to be used exclusively by grown-ups. The problem was that the factory workers and farmers didn't use it much and within a year it fell apart. The books were donated to the ministerial library at the church.

OK, now we have to digress and talk about the Dartmouth case. This'll all come together, I promise.

In 1821, the state tried to take over Dartmouth College and establish a state university there.

Daniel Webster defended the school and convinced the New

Hampshire Supreme Court that it did not have the power to take over an entity simply 'cause it wanted to.

So the state had to go pound sand, as it were. It was humiliating. Also the state had raised all this money to found a university. What to do with the money? Well, the legislature voted to divide the money and give it back to the towns. The money, they said, was raised for education and the towns could use it to support the schools, or (and this is crucial), they could use it for "other purposes of education."

So, at the town meeting of 1833, Rev. Abbott said that this "other purposes of education" could mean purchasing books for a town library and he had a great start already with the juvenile library and the now-defunct "Peterborough Library Company."

"OK," the voters said. "Look, we'll put most of the money back into the schools, but we'll put a few bucks aside for the library and, (and this is important) "we will put a few bucks in from the general coffers."

And thus was formed the first free town-supported public library. At the time, no one knew anything historical was taking place. No one thought anything about it.

And, by the way, the whole scheme may have been illegal, but it was never tested.

It would be 16 more years before the state legislature would authorize towns to use tax money for town libraries. And incidentally, not only would Peterborough have the first tax-supported library, New Hampshire would be the first state in the union to pass such a law. England would pass a similar law a year later and Massachusetts two years later.

The books continued to be housed at the church or the parsonage. It would be 60 years before the library building itself would be constructed. It opened in 1893.

But the idea of a public-supported library endured . . . and so did many of the original books. They are housed in a special case there and can be seen any time the library is open. ❧

Purgatory Rock

PURGATORY ROCK IN Mont Vernon was once one of the most visited and popular attractions in New Hampshire.

For fifty years, back in the 19th century, there was a day in late summer when the towns of Mont Vernon and Lyndeborough used to get together at the rock to hold a grand picnic.

It was the highlight of the year. And at one time there was a dance floor and a bowling alley, picnic tables and a place to play baseball.

All that is now gone. What used to be fields are now woods. You can't drive in there anymore; you have to hike. The place now looks much like it must have when it was first discovered back in the 1700s.

Then it was a place of legend, a haunted place. Parents told their children scary tales about this place to keep them in line.

The reason is that, above the waterfall, is a giant footprint outlined in the stone. It is said the devil himself stood there and the heat of his foot burned this print into the solid granite. And there, beside the footprint, is a deep spherical hole carved into the same stone. The inside is shaped like a pot and it is said the devil once made a meal there. This is the Devil's Bean Pot.

The stream there is the Black Brook. Downstream are the Pulpit, the Overhanging Rock, the Devil's Den, and the Old Boy's Face. One side of the brook is Mont Vernon and the other side is Lyndeborough. It is, of course, one of many chasms formed by the glacial outwash. It is not unlike Pulpit Rock in Bedford, or Sculpture Rock in Groton, or Chesterfield Gorge in Chesterfield.

Back before the Civil War, there were very few trees in southern New Hampshire. Most of it was farm and field, all cleared. It was easier to get to the rock then.

When the railroads expanded after the Civil War, people came from Boston. They arrived in Milford and took a wagon up to the village and on to the wonderful Mont Vernon Hotel. With no trees, the view was spectacular. And it was much cooler than the city, and close enough so mom and the kids could spend the week there and dad would come up on the train for the weekends.

'Course the guests of the hotel needed activity and Purgatory was a perfect place to visit. And in 1898, some local entrepreneurs expanded the area. It was then that the bowling alley and dance floor was put in. The business lasted until about World War I.

After that the automobile came in and people stopped going to the grand hotels.

When I was a Boy Scout back in the 1940s, we used to hike up there. It was one of the great places to visit. Still is. ⚓

Sanbornton

A GREAT MANY of the towns in New Hampshire are what are called Masonian Grant towns.

These are the places that were settled or resettled in the mid-1700s by a bunch of developers over in Portsmouth. These men claimed a great many of the towns in the state under the auspice of a grant made to the grandfather of one of their founders, John Mason. It was the biggest land grab in the state's history.

One of the first of these Masonian towns was Sanbornton. And in 1748, New Hampshire's first colonial governor, Benning Wentworth, gave the place its charter and called it after some of the first settlers. I say "some" because, of the sixty people granted land, a full dozen were named Sanborn.

And, by the by, one of the first Sanborns to settle here was married to Ann Bachiler, the daughter of the Reverend Stephen Bachiler, who was perhaps the most controversial person in New Hampshire during the 17th century.

He was an old guy (in his seventies) when he was charged with adultery. And his fourth wife had children with another man, a guy from Kittery, and was whipped as an adulterer and branded with an "A."

Anyhow, Ann Bachiler was married to a Sanborn for whom this town is named.

And, incidentally, the first name for the town was not as it is now, Sanbornton, but rather Sanborntown.

The place was already known because a couple years before a bunch of militiamen, under the command of Colonel Theodore Atkinson, had built a winter fort near what is now Sanbornton Bridge. The fort was to protect the towns in the southern part of New Hampshire from attack from the French and Indians during what was called the "Canada Expedition."

The town was officially incorporated under the last Colonial governor, John Wentworth, in 1770. It was then that the name was modified to Sanbornton.

A lot of history there! ✒

Sharon Schoolhouse

UP UNTIL WORLD WAR II, most towns in America had small, one-room schoolhouses built in various parts of their communities.

Kids, of course, attended the closest one because they had to walk to school. Often there would be a dozen or so students in the school of various ages—all taught by one teacher.

Most of these schools have nowadays been torn down or converted to residences or antique shops. The little red schoolhouse over in Jaffrey Center has been restored as a museum of sorts. There is a perfectly preserved one-room schoolhouse over in East Andover that practically no one knows about.

But my favorite schoolhouse is in Sharon, New Hampshire.

It looks just about the way it did in 1900. Nowadays it is used as a polling place and for town meetings. It is Sharon's only large public building.

Back in the 1890s, John Taggert went to this school, and he writes about it in the *Sharon Town History*. Back then there were three schoolhouses in Sharon.

The present-day one took in the district known as Sharon City. John writes that there were 50 students there in the wintertime and half that number attended in the summer.

"There were," he tells us, "two sections of homemade white-pine seats in the school . . . one side for boys . . . one side for girls.

"A common punishment was to seat a boy on the girls' side or a girl on the boys' side. (More boys sat on the girls' side than vice versa.)

"In the middle of the school sat a large box stove, a 'schoolhouse' stove, that took extra-long pieces of wood. The stovepipe ran to the furthermost wall chimney so that every calorie of heat was extracted before it got outside. In the summer, the stove often was opened at the top and filled with blossoms like a giant flowerpot.

"One teacher taught all eight grades at the same time.

"Spelling matches were popular, the boys often against the girls. The 'three R's were stressed but also algebra, chemistry, geography . . . even one time and one particular teacher . . . astronomy.

"The school had no running water. There was an outhouse.

"And Uncle Billy Livingston lived just down the road, and he had a drinking trough by the roadside . . . one side was for horses . . . the other side for people, and there was a tin dipper there for public use.

"It was considered a treat and a privilege to be allowed to go for a drink of water from the school."

John Taggert writes that at graduation Deacon Moore always gave the commencement address, and never failed to stress the same message year after year.

His advice was, "It is always better to aim high and miss the mark . . . than to aim low and hit it."

Good advice. ☙

Sunapee Named

TO BEGIN WITH, the town was called after the English Secretary of War, George Saville.

Saville was a great supporter of the American Colonies. He was one of the few Englishmen of power to try to prevent the American Revolution. Saville Row, the clothing and tailoring section of London, was also named after Sir George.

So in the original charter, granted in 1768, this place was named Saville.

One of the grantees and first settlers of the town was a man named Oliver Corey. He had fought the French in Canada and later fought in the Revolution. The section of town where he lived was called "Corey's town."

Also among the first half dozen or so grantees were General John Sullivan of Revolutionary fame and Mathew Thornton, who signed the Declaration of Independence.

A second grant of the town was given to the Masonian Proprietors in 1772. And the town was renamed yet again; this time for John Wendell, one of the proprietors.

And Wendell it stayed for the next 78 years, until the official incorporation of the town in 1850. At this time, Governor Samuel Dinsmore Jr. and the legislature decided that the town should be at one with the mountain that overlooks it and the lake it was on, and they re-christened the town "Sunapee."

So there you have it, four names: Saville, Coreystown, Wendell and, finally, Sunapee.

Sunapee, I think you may know, is an Algonquin Indian name taken from two words.

The first word is "Soona" which is the word for "goose." The second word is "apee" which means "lake."

I, for one, am pleased that they chose the more romantic Indian name, Sunapee. ✏

Surry

THE TOWN WAS called Surry for the English town of the same name. It is not a large place.

But small as it is, this town has some wonderful places to visit and some wonderful stories as well.

Much of the town—case you didn't know—was moved there from somewhere else.

Like the town of Hill, the U.S. Army built a Corps of Engineers' dam there back in the 1940s, and lots of old farms had to be moved or torn down to make way for the lake and the flood plain. Nowadays the farmland is being renewed by the Corps and brought back to the fertile condition it once had.

What the town got for its agony is the body of water where people come to swim and picnic and boat and fish. It is truly a hidden treasure.

Up on Surry Mountain over the years, there were quarries and mines. One enterprising gentleman once raised money to make a goldmine. Seems he loaded a shotgun with pellets of gold and fired into an embankment upon the hillside and then went up with prospective investors who, of course, found the gold and invested. The swindler took their money and fled.

Way up where the swale is between two peaks . . . kinda a saddle part . . . there is a tiny swampy pond that has been measured to be 70 feet deep in one part. It just goes down like an inverted cone.

And back behind the town offices, there is a gravestone of a benefactor of the town who is remembered, not for what he did for the community, but simply for his name. And no, he never knew Washington Irving of "Sleepy Hollow"; he died before it was even written.

But his name will make you smile . . . "Ichabod Crane." ❧

Christmas in New Hampshire

ALL OVER THE world, when people think of Christmas, they think of New Hampshire.

All over the world, the average Christmas card shows a sleigh and horses . . . shows lights shining from an old farmhouse across a snow-covered meadow . . . shows a covered bridge.

The face of Christmas is a Currier and Ives print . . . and the Currier and Ives corner of America is the Monadnock region of New Hampshire. Ask a school child in Nairobi, Kenya, or Dublin, Ireland, to draw a picture of Christmas and, more likely than not, they will draw, from memory, a scene in New Hampshire.

And, yes, New England itself is Christmas, too. But often Massachusetts and Connecticut won't have snow for the holidays. But Vermont will have snow at Christmas . . . and Maine will have snow at Christmas, and New Hampshire.

Draw an "X" connecting the four corners of New England and the center of that "X" will fall just outside Wilton Center . . . New Hampshire. We are *the* geographical heart of New England.

Oh, yes, in our minds there are Victorian singers on the streets of London and Tiny Tim God Blessing everyone. . . .

And there are chromium tinsel trees in the malls in Miami Beach and thousands of kids celebrating St. Nick on the rides at Disneyland. And in Australia and Argentina it is mid-summer.

But the ideal Christmas morning lies in the heart of New England. In New Hampshire. ❧

THE PEOPLE

Jesse Buters in the Snow

ON FEBRUARY 25, 1829, it snowed and snowed. All day, all night.

Jesse Buters lived on a farm in Jaffrey over on the Rindge border. He needed to go to town for supplies and so borrowed a horse at the Litch Homestead, who were neighbors living about half a mile down the road.

Jesse got his errands done but, because of the snow, he got back to the Litch Homestead after dark. He wiped the horse down and put it in its stall and started the last half-mile walk home. But the storm was fierce and, by then, the snow was better than knee deep.

The next day, the people on the farm where Jesse lived trudged over to the Litch place to find Jesse, because he had not yet come home. They supposed he had spent the night there.

He had not, and hundreds of searchers went looking for him. It should be easy, they thought. It was only half a mile between the two places. But no, there was no sign of the man. Just miles of deep snow.

Weeks passed and then months. People wondered if he was in the river or had run away. People talked of nothing else.

And then spring came. And on a day in April, two young ladies who lived in the area, Polly Stevens and Lucy Kimball, decided to go out for a walk. They joked and used the remark people were saying when they went walking. They said, "We're going out to find Jesse Buters."

As they came up the hill toward the Litch farm, they looked over the stone wall and there, under a large maple tree, was Jesse. He was sitting in the snow. Just his head and shoulders were visible. He had been sitting there all winter, covered over with snow.

When they dug him out, he appeared to be smiling and by his side was a bottle of rum . . . partly consumed.

And that's the story, except some of the old-timers who live in Jaffrey, when they wanna go out for a walk, they don't say it outright, they say, "Well, I guess I'll go find Jesse Buters." ♣

Salmon Portland Chase

IF YOU COME up Route 12 to the town of Cornish, you will probably note a New Hampshire state marker identifying the town as the birthplace of Salmon Portland Chase.

Salmon Portland Chase. It is one of those names that seem familiar and yet, hard to identify. Something to do with the Civil War, you think . . . something to do with Abraham Lincoln.

And if you think that, you are right; Salmon P. Chase did have a lot to do with Honest Abe.

Chase is responsible for something else. Something that you look at most every day and probably take for granted. Something that pleases many people. But something that infuriates many other people. Any idea what this is? If you don't have a clue, I'll tell you later.

Now Salmon P. Chase was an amazing guy, and, yes, he was born in Cornish.

His grand-daddy was one of the original settlers of the town. Back then families had lots of kids. Salmon's grand-daddy had fourteen kids. One of those kids, Salmon's uncle, was Philander Chase.

Philander Chase single-handedly founded Kenyan College out in Ohio and was, in his time, the best-known Episcopalian bishop in America. I think today, it might be argued, New Hampshire's Bishop Gene Robinson has more world-wide celebrity. But back then it was Philander. That being neither here nor there, I just wanted to note that the Chase family were shakers and movers.

Salmon (and, you know, I don't know if the "L" is pronounced in the name . . . and what kind of name "Salmon" is anyway. I find it fishy. Or for that matter, what kind of name is "Philander"?) . . . Anyhow, Salmon was born in Cornish on the 13th of January, 1808. He was the eighth of eleven kids.

Now the family didn't stay in Cornish very long. When Salmon was six, his dad moved the family to Keene. So Salmon went to elementary school in Keene. At sixteen he went off to study law at Dartmouth College. He graduated in 1826 and, like his Uncle Philander, moved west to Ohio.

There he was a success in the law and, in 1849, he became a U.S.

senator from the Buckeye State. Six years later, Salmon Chase became Ohio's first Republican governor.

Now Governor Chase was a personable guy, a darn good politician, and as smart a man as you'd want to meet. Abe Lincoln was one of his biggest fans and, when the Civil War broke out in 1861, Lincoln called on his friend to be Secretary of the Treasury.

In this job it fell to Salmon P. Chase to find the money to prosecute the war. This was the most important political position there was. And a more difficult job would be hard to imagine. Salmon Chase pulled it off brilliantly.

See, up to that time there was only gold and silver coinage. Paper money was printed only for individual state banks. But if the bank went belly up, the paper money from that bank was often worthless. People didn't trust paper money.

Chase changed all that. He did this by founding the first National Banks. These banks marketed huge bond issues to finance the war . . . backed, of course, by the full credit of the United States itself (at least the Union side of the United States). And, not incidentally, because the federal government stood behind these banks, the paper money was trusted as well.

This national banking system stayed in place for about forty years, until the establishment of the Federal Reserve System in 1903.

Anyhow, Abe Lincoln was so pleased with his friend's work that he appointed him Chief Justice of the Supreme Court.

Salmon Chase replaced the late Justice Roger Tanney who, you may remember, was the author of the Dred Scott decision. Briefly, this decision concluded that slaves owned in the South were still slaves, even if their masters brought them North to a non-slave state. This was one of the most shameful court decisions in American history. It was one of the reasons, some think, for the Civil War itself.

And, by the way, Chief Justice Chase was the one who administered the oath of office to Lincoln at his second inauguration.

OK, now for that thing I told you I'd tell you about; that thing that will forever remind you of this man.

This is it. Money.

Ever wonder why and when we have the motto "In God We Trust" on every piece of United States coinage or paper money?

Well, you got it.

It was, in fact, Salmon Portland Chase who decreed it back in 1863, during the war. A minister in rural Pennsylvania suggested it and Salmon Chase loved the idea. The motto first appeared on the two-cent piece in 1864, and it has been on all our money ever since.

One other thing; after Salmon Portland Chase died in 1873, a bank was founded in New York and named for him . . . you got it . . . the Chase Manhattan Bank, one of the mightiest financial institutions in the world.

So there you have it.

Next time you hand a dollar over for a cup of coffee think about the motto "In God We Trust" and think of Salmon Chase . . . and tell him what you think about it. ❧

Winston Churchill

WHO WAS THE most popular novelist in America at the turn of the 20th century?

I'll give you a hint. He lived in Cornish, New Hampshire.

If you live in Cornish, you know I am speaking of Winston Churchill.

I know, Sir Winston never lived in Cornish. That's a fact. This was a different Winston Churchill who spelled his name just the same as the English statesman-to-be.

But if, in 1899, you had asked most anyone in America (or in England, for that matter) who Winston Churchill was, they would tell you he was the author who wrote the novels *The Celebrity* and *Richard Carvel*.

New Hampshire's Winston Churchill was wildly popular. He was the Danielle Steele of his time both here and abroad. His stuff, by the way, was pretty trashy but it was good fun to read. In fact, it is still good fun to read.

And he made a lot of money. Enough, in fact, to commission architect Charles Platt to design a grand mansion on a bluff facing Mt. Ascutney with the Connecticut River in the foreground. He called his estate after his wife's maiden name, "Harlakenden."

"Harlakenden" was to become world-famous in 1913, '14 and '15, when it was rented by President Woodrow Wilson. In those years, it became one of the first so-called "Summer White Houses." But that's a story for another time.

At Harlakenden, Winston Churchill wrote a dozen or more novels over the years.

And Winston Churchill, like his English counterpart, loved politics. He represented the town of Cornish in the state legislature for a number of years. Later he became a state senator.

In 1908, he tried for the Republican nomination for governor. His platform was the reform of the legislature, which was, many people say, owned outright by the Boston and Main Railroad. Candidate Churchill missed being nominated by only 52 votes.

Our Winston Churchill loved Teddy Roosevelt. He, in fact, knew him personally. Teddy used to visit Cornish and, on such occasions, Churchill wined and dined him.

In 1912, Churchill ran for governor again, this time as a Bull Moose candidate. This was another nod to Teddy Roosevelt who had created the party. But, like his hero, Teddy, Churchill lost the general election big time.

Although he did not reform the legislature and oust the Boston and Main Railroad influence, he did write a book about the scandal. He called it "Conniston," and it became the number-one best seller in America. Through this book, the entire country was told of the shenanigans at the New Hampshire State House.

I know, I haven't answered your first question, of course. That is the one you immediately thought of, which is: Did Sir Winston Churchill and author Winston Churchill ever meet?

The answer is, yes. They met in Boston in 1899. The English Winston Churchill wrote that the Cornish Winston Churchill threw a party for him in the Bean City.

"Some confusion persisted," the English Churchill wrote, "all of my mails were sent to his address and the bill for dinner came to me." Also there were a number of letters between the two Winstons, where the English Winston has a solution to their name problem:

"Mr. Winston Churchill," Mr. Winston Churchill writes from England, "will recognize, from this letter, if indeed by no other means, that there is a grave danger of his works being mistaken for those of Mr. Winston Churchill. He feels sure that Mr. Winston Churchill desires this as little as he does himself. In future to avoid mistakes as much as possible, Mr. Winston Churchill has decided to sign all published articles 'Winston Spencer Churchill' and not 'Winston Churchill' as formerly."

He later suggested that our Winston Churchill sign his works as "Winston Churchill, The American," which he never did. ✒

Cigar Box John

DERRY, OF COURSE, is known all over the world for being the boy-hood home of astronaut Alan Shepard and for being the place where Robert Frost lived and wrote much of his best poetry.

Derry, New Hampshire, is a place rich in American history and a place where many important people have done important things.

Take for instance, Captain John Laycock.

Captain Laycock first bought a home in Derry in 1934. He retired there ten years later. In the interim he was responsible for two of the great inventions of World War II . . . the Quonset hut . . . and the pontoon bridge.

Captain Laycock was also the commander of the Boston Navy Yard and friends with Franklin Roosevelt and his civil works adminis-trator and good friend and advisor, Harry Hopkins.

The pontoons that John Laycock developed were proven right in Derry, just before the start of the war. These devices were, in effect, welded steel boxes five feet by five feet by seven feet. They were hooked together to make floating bridges that would support even the heavi-est tanks. They were simple, quick, and inexpensive to manufacture; easy to assemble and disassemble and elegant in design.

They also made wonderfully strong piers for landing supplies going to the front. The military first used them in the landings on Sicily where they caught the German Army completely off guard.

Captain Laycock tested out his design of these pontoons over on Beaver Lake while vacationing with his family. His first prototypes were cigar boxes wired or nailed together. He even used these same cigar boxes when he demonstrated his idea to officials of the U.S. Navy in Washington D.C.

The Navy was charmed and gave Captain Laycock their complete support. They also gave him a nickname. A nickname that stuck.

To the end of his life, Captain Laycock was called by all who knew him, "Cigar Box John."

Mary Corliss' Cheese

THERE IS A story told in the town of Alexandria about a woman whose life and home were saved by cheese.

The woman saved by a cheese was Mary Corliss.

Mary and her husband John had emigrated to Alexandria from Northern Ireland back in the early 1700s. Alexandria was then the frontier.

There in the wilderness the couple built a cabin and cleared the land for their two cows and a couple pigs, chickens and geese. John went to the trouble of digging a deep cellar hole for the house. It was, at the time, the only home in the town to have a basement.

Little did John know that this cellar would, one day, along with the cheese, save his wife's life.

The years went by and the Corlisses had two strapping sons.

One day the men of the family were out in the fields. Mary, alone in the cabin, looked out to see a number of Indians among the trees. She was in danger and so were the family's cattle.

As the Indians approached the house, Mary went to the stairway that lead to the cellar. Here at the top of the stairs were shelves that held half a dozen large cheese rounds.

Mary called down the stairs as if the men were there.

"Come on, boys!" she yelled, and threw a cheese down the stairway. It made a noise as if someone were running up the stairs.

"Bam, bam, bam," a second cheese went down the stairway.

"Come, John!" Mary called, and threw another cheese.

This she did until all the cheeses were at the foot of the stairs. She then looked out to see that the Indians had vanished.

Apparently they had decided that too many men were within the cabin to risk an attack.

And so it was that a woman saved a home and her cattle. And yes, her family was still able to eat the cheese. ❧

Lady Di

BEDFORD. DID YOU know that the town was named for the husband of Lady Diana Spencer? Well, it was.

See, first off, all this area was a part of Massachusetts and was called simply, Narragansett Number Five.

It got the name because the land was granted to a group of men who had fought in the early French and Indian Wars in battles against the Narragansett Indians in Rhode Island. But these veterans did not settle there. Rather, they sold their grants to speculators.

Governor John Belcher of Massachusetts then granted it to these men and renamed this place Souhegan East, after the river over in what is now the Milford-Amherst area.

Then New Hampshire became its own colony and that's when Governor Benning Wentworth again granted the place to his friends, and renamed it Bedford as homage to his friend Lord John Russel, who was the Earl of Bedford.

Governor Benning and the Earl of Bedford were great friends from the time they were young men together in England. Benning Wentworth was a trader of rum and timber, sugar and slaves, and his friend the Earl later became the Lord of the Admiralty.

It was all politics back then, as it is now, and Governor Wentworth was just kissing up.

The Earl of Bedford, by the way, later became Secretary of State under George II, an even more powerful post.

It was John Goffe, one of the founders of Bedford, who petitioned Governor Wentworth for the creation of the town.

Oh yes, you are no doubt wondering what Lady Di has to do with Bedford.

Well, Lady Diana Spencer was the cousin of the Duke of Marlboro and the wife of the Earl of Bedford.

No, this was not the Lady Diana Spencer who married Charles. This was the much older Lady Diana Spencer for whom the 20th century Lady Di was named.

But I found the fact curious and thought you might, too. ❧

The Fife Revolver

IN THE NORTH PEMBROKE CEMETERY is the grave of a man named Harmon Fife.

I know, it says Harmon Fife on the gravestone but that, it turns out, is a misspelling. It is an ironic postscript, for poor Harmon Fife never did get the consideration he was due.

For Harmon Fife invented the revolver.

I know, Samuel Colt invented the revolver. The Colt-45 won the West. All the legendary gunfighters from Billy the Kid to the Jesse James gang used Colt-45 revolvers.

So where does Harmon Fife come in here?

Well, in 1835 in Pembroke, he made a revolver by hand. His design worked by squeezing on the trigger guard to advance the cylinder with a new bullet and then putting the finger in the trigger to fire the gun.

A lot of people thought that Sam Colt stole the idea for his gun from Fife. The fact is though that both men came up with their designs about the same time. The Colt advanced the cylinder by cocking the gun. That's why the gunfighters fanned their guns; that is, slammed the hammer back with their free hand so they could fire again and again. Anyone using Fife's design was at a clear disadvantage.

On Harmon Fife's grave the verse reads:

> *Here lies the man never beat by a plan*
> *Straight was his aim and sure of his game*
> *Never was a lover, but invented the revolver.* ☙

First to Climb Monadnock

THE FIRST WHITE man ever to climb Mt. Monadnock was also the first to visit what is now Peterborough village. He came to this area to kill Indians.

In 1723, one Reverend Joseph Willard was killed by four Indians in his home in Rutland, Massachusetts. His scalp was taken to Quebec where it was redeemed for money.

Reverend Willard's cousin, Samuel Willard, was a captain in the Massachusetts Militia. Captain Willard lived in Lancaster, Massachusetts, and, because of the brutality of his uncle's killing, he vowed vengeance on all Native Americans.

In July of 1725, Captain Willard, with fifty-two men of his community and five friendly Indians, set out from Lancaster. They had volunteered to go north to put down Indian uprisings.

On July 31, his diary records that he and fourteen men camped "on ye top of Wannadnuck Mountain." (And, yes, that's "Wannadnuck" spelled with a "W.") And thus happened the first recorded ascent of Monadnock.

Later the party walked up the Contoocook River and, on the second of August, arrived at the confluence of the Contoocook and Nubanusit streams. And this was the first recorded visit of a European American to this area now called Peterborough.

By the way, no Native Americans were encountered on this trip. ❧

First Death on Mount Washington

HE WAS A robust young man. A little arrogant. But that came naturally; after all, he was the son of a British peer.

Sir George Strickland was a member of Parliament. His son, Frederick, would, no doubt, follow in his footsteps. For the moment, however, Frederick was traveling . . . seeing the world and in the height of the foliage season was at an inn in New Hampshire's White Mountains.

This was a long time ago . . . back before the Civil War, 1851 to be exact.

As I said, it was late fall. The foliage was bright and the mountains were dusted with snow. Frederick was staying at Abel Crawford's Inn. The day dawned clear and the young Englishman noted that he wished to climb Mt. Washington.

"Not today," he was told. "Too dangerous and too slippery and the weather might break any second."

"Nonsense," the young man said. Why, he could see the summit. He could get up and down easily. He had climbed the Alps. This would be a piece of cake.

One of the guides at the inn said that he would lead Frederick up the hill, but only to show him that it couldn't be done on such a day. The two set off. By the time they had reached the top of Mt. Clinton, there was a steady light snow and the wind was blowing.

"Time to head back," the guide said.

"Well, I will persevere!" the young peer said. And trudged off.

The guide turned back, certain that the young man would soon become discouraged and do the same. But Frederick Strickland did not turn back.

The following morning a party ventured out from the inn. At the top of Mt. Clinton, they picked up the young man's tracks. The hiker started up the main trail but soon had diverged to a more direct route straight up the mountainside.

Soon they found pieces of ripped clothing and blood on the trail, indications that the lad had fallen down some steep precipices and was hurt.

Then in the Valley of the Amanoosuk, they found him face down in a little stream. He was nearly naked and bloody. He had broken bones and was bruised and frozen solid.

They carried him back to the inn.

The body of Frederick Strickland was shipped back to Bridlington, England, where it was interred.

His was the first recorded death ever on Mt. Washington. ❧

First Shot at Lexington

IN DEERING IS the grave of the man who, it is said, fired "The shot heard 'round the world."

His name was Ebenezer Locke. If you think about it, of course someone had to fire the first shot at the battle of Lexington; the actual first shot that began the American Revolution. And Ebenezer Locke claims to have been that man.

But, before you get too excited about this, let me say, there is a caveat here. This may not be the guy. The only written account we have of that first shot is in the records of Middlesex County in Massachusetts. It is an affidavit filed in 1840 by Amos Locke, the first cousin of Ebenezer. Amos tells us that he and his cousin Ebenezer lived at that time in Lexington. It was there they heard that the British were on the march. The cousins went to the meetinghouse. There they were informed that it was a false alarm. There were no soldiers on the march.

And so they started back home. But soon they came across a man named Asabel Porter of Woburn. Porter had been shot through the body. A short distance away was a line of British soldiers. It was then that Ebenezer took aim and fired his musket.

The troops formed into a line and the cousins fell back, carrying the wounded man.

Now this is the oldest recorded statement there is regarding the battle. And because it is written down, Ebenezer Locke has the best claim to being the man who fired "The shot heard 'round the world."

Before you get too excited, let me tell you that, it turns out, there were *two* Ebenezer Lockes in the town of Lexington, a younger and an older. Both men shared the same grandfather, one William Locke, of Woburn.

The roster from the battle of Lexington, however, shows that there was only one Ebenezer Locke at the battle. He was in Colonel Parker's Company.

The question is, was it this Ebenezer, or his cousin? No one knows. We do know this Ebenezer moved his family to New Hampshire, but we don't know when. We also know he claimed to the day he died that he had fired that first shot. But there is no solid proof that the Ebenezer Locke in the affidavit by Amos Locke is this man. And there is another question which you probably thought of, too, and that is, when the cousins discovered Asabel Porter, the wounded man, why was he wounded?

Doesn't it seem more likely that it was Asabel Porter who fired the first shot? Naw, Ebenezer is the guy! ✎

Edward Gove

DID YOU EVER hear of Edward Gove?

Well, Edward Gove is New Hampshire's first great Independence hero. He was a guy who dared to take a stand. And he put his life and fortune on the line against the forces of tyranny.

Let me tell you the story.

This all started because of a grant of land made by the British Crown to a guy named John Mason. That grant was for much of what is now New Hampshire. In fact, it was Mason who named it "New Hampshire," after the county of Hampshire where he lived in England.

But Mason died before he could develop his grant.

His grandson, however, saw a killing to be made by reviving the grant and making all the settlers in New Hampshire, in effect, re-purchase their farms from him . . . and pay taxes to him.

First, though, he had to convince the King that the people of New Hampshire wanted him to be in control.

New Hampshire was then part of Massachusetts, so the first order of the day was to have the province separated from its control from Boston. To do this a man was sent to England to tell the King that the citizens of New Hampshire hated Massachusetts and wanted out.

The direct opposite was the case, however. The citizens of Hampton and Portsmouth and Dover had all voted their allegiance to Boston and their hatred of this Masonian land grab.

But King James II heard only one side and he made New Hampshire its own colony. He appointed Edward Cranfield governor of the new Masonian province. And here's where Edward Gove comes in.

Gove was a landowner in Hampton and a popular guy. He was hard drinking and spoke his mind. And Edward Gove let it be known that he regarded Cranfield as a pretended governor. Gove said that his commission had been signed in Scotland, and James II was a papist and that all this was null and void. Further, Edward Gove declared that his sword was drawn.

Governor Cranfield responded by issuing an arrest warrant for Gove and he called out the militia. The militia went to Exeter where

Gove appeared at the head of a dozen men, all mounted with swords and pistols and muskets. They also had a trumpeter who sounded the attack as the men charged the militia.

It was over in a nonce. No one was hurt, but all except the trumpeter were arrested. The trumpeter made a getaway. The dozen or so prisoners were taken in irons to Portsmouth where, one at a time, they appeared before the governor and council.

Gove told the council that the governor was "no judge of the court, but a pretended one, and a traitor to the king and his authority."

All the men were committed to jail at New Castle. All were charged with high treason.

On Monday, February 15, 1683, the men appeared before a local court. Most pleaded "not guilty" and sentiment was with them. All but Gove were acquitted.

Gove alone was convicted of treason. His sentence was harsh, quote: "That he should be drawn to the place of execution, and there be hanged by the neck and cut down alive, and that his entrails be taken out and burnt before his face and his head cut off, and this body divided into four quarters, and his head and quarters disposed of at the King's pleasure."

But feeling was high in favor of Edward Gove, and he was reprieved.

Instead of death, he was sent to England and locked in the Tower of London for three years, after which he received a full pardon. He returned to Hampton, where he lived out his life without incident. ❧

John Parker Hale

OUTSIDE THE NEW HAMPSHIRE STATEHOUSE in Concord, there are four statues of famous men: Daniel Webster, President Franklin Pierce, General John Stark, and Senator John Parker Hale.

Most school children in New Hampshire could tell you something about Webster or Pierce or Stark, but even few adults could tell you a thing about John Parker Hale. And this is odd because in his time he was one of the most controversial men in America.

In 1843, John Parker Hale was elected as the U.S. Congressman from New Hampshire. Hale was a Democrat.

This was a day and age when neither the Democrats nor the Whig Party stood publicly against slavery. But John Parker Hale took a firm stand in favor of abolition. He was a fine speaker and his speeches were printed in newspapers and quoted by abolitionists all over the country. This made him dangerous to the balance of power in the country. The Democratic party tried to hold their representative in check but Hale would have none of it.

All this came to a head in 1845 when Hale broke with his party to vote against the annexation of Texas. He did that because Texas would be slave holding.

At the time of his vote, John Parker Hale was standing for re-election.

The Democrats were so incensed by his action that they called a special convention to take back his candidacy and drum him out of the party. As a Democrat, John Parker Hale's career was over.

But John Parker Hale was not one to stay down.

Instead, he and others started their own party, the "Independent Democrats." Under their banner Hale stumped the state and got himself elected to the New Hampshire House of Representatives as speaker.

Now this was a time when U.S. senators were not directly elected. Instead, the state legislatures voted who would become a U.S. senator, and John Parker Hale was sent to Washington as a senator from New Hampshire. He was the first and the only antislavery person in the entire Senate.

To say he was hated by the southern senators is to understate the case.

Senator Albert Brown of Mississippi said that if Hale were ever to come to his state he would find himself hanging from a tree with a rope around his neck and, if necessary, he would assist in the operation.

Poet John Greenleaf Whittier, however, wrote of Senator Hale:

> God bless New Hampshire, from her granite peaks
> Once more the voice of Stark and Langdon speaks. . . .

But until the Civil War, John Parker Hale was virtually alone in his crusade against slavery. After the war, lots of politicians decided to become brave.

In 1852, Hale joined the "Free Soil Party" and ran for president. His opponent was Franklin Pierce, who, of course, won. But here was an election where two of the candidates came from the same state, New Hampshire.

At the close of the Civil War and, in fact, the very afternoon before his assassination, Abraham Lincoln appointed John Parker Hale as ambassador to Spain.

Some say he went to Spain to protect his daughter from a great scandal.

But that is another story. ✍

Lucy Hale

SHE WAS PLUMP and jolly. She was a flirt, and she was headstrong. No one, it seems, could do anything about her.

She had been wooed by Oliver Wendell Holmes, Jr. She had turned him down.

And Abraham Lincoln himself hoped that she would marry his son Robert. For Robert Todd Lincoln also was smitten by her. He had met her here in New Hampshire when he had been a student at Phillips Exeter Academy.

But she had given her heart to a person who was not her social equal.

Her love, in fact, was for an actor!

The young woman we are talking about was Lucy Hale of Dover. She was the daughter of a U.S. senator from New Hampshire, John Parker Hale.

John Parker Hale was the most rabid antislavery man in the entire U.S. Senate. He was a gifted speaker and an in-your-face confrontationist. He made hundreds of enemies in the Congress. But he was way out in front of the crowd in his opposition to slavery. Some called him foolhardy; some called him the bravest man in Washington, D.C. Some Southern senators had publicly said that they wished him dead.

During the Civil War, John Parker Hale's daughter Lucy became more and more unmanageable. By the end of the war, she had been seen in public places, holding hands and kissing her lover, the matinee idol. She had, in fact, given the actor a ruby ring as an engagement gift.

To get her away from her love affair, John Parker Hale, who was no longer a senator, went to Abraham Lincoln and begged an ambassadorship to Spain. He would take Lucy with him, he said, and thus away from that scoundrel actor. Perhaps after they came back, she might marry Robert Lincoln.

Lucy had, earlier that week, told her lover that her father intended to spirit her away from him.

The President granted Hale the ambassadorship. That was done the very afternoon of the day Lincoln would be killed at Ford's Theater, April 14, 1865.

Later that week the Hales debarked for Europe with Lucy.

And the actor?

The actor was John Wilkes Booth, the man who shot the President.

On April 24, Booth was shot at the Garrett Farm in Maryland while running from a burning barn.

As he lay dying, John Wilkes Booth was paralyzed and asked to have his hands lifted so he could see them. He died looking at Lucy's ring.

His last words were unintelligible. They were written down as "useless, useless," but many think his last words were, "Lucy, Lucy."

Lucy, by the way, returned from Spain and married, not Robert Todd Lincoln, but William Chandler who, like her father, was a U.S. senator from New Hampshire. ✒

Sarah Josepha Hale

SARAH BEUELL WAS born on a farm in Newport, New Hampshire, in 1788; a long time ago.

It was a time when few women were formally educated, and Sarah was no exception. But when her brother, Horatio, went to Dartmouth, he brought home his books and lessons and through him she too learned the classics. Later she became a schoolteacher in a time when most teachers were men.

She married a lawyer from Newport, a man named David Hale. The couple had five children.

But David caught a chill coming home in a carriage one winter evening and got pneumonia and died. He left his family with nothing.

To support her family, Sarah tried the millinery business . . . and she wrote. And in 1822 she authored a book that became a best seller. It was set in New Hampshire and was called after the town it took place in, *Northwood*.

Northwood preceded *Uncle Toms Cabin* and, like that novel, *Northwood* was a tale of slavery and emancipation.

With *Northwood*, Sarah Josepha Hale secured her reputation. As a result, she was picked to be the editor of the largest women's magazine in America, *Godey's Ladies' Book*.

It is hard to exaggerate the influence this magazine had in this country. It was the arbiter of fashion and of taste and the most important publication advocating the education of women. By Civil War time, Sarah Josepha Hale was one of the most influential women in America.

During this time, Sarah Josepha Hale also edited a book of children's poems, and in this book was the verse, "Mary Had A Little Lamb." She did not write the verse but she is credited with its wide publication and popularity.

"Mary's Little Lamb" aside, Sarah Josepha Hale also had great cause to which she gave almost twenty years of her life. She wanted the United States to have an official day of thanksgiving. She editorialized for the creation of the day and she wrote and spoke with many important people of the day about its creation.

But in 1863, right at the start of the Civil War, Sarah Josepha Hale had a conversation with President Abraham Lincoln and Lincoln was moved by her idea.

As a result he proclaimed the last Thursday in November would henceforth be an official National Day of Thanksgiving.

A Thursday was chosen, I am told, because the first officially proclaimed Thanksgiving Day was a Thursday. I say, officially proclaimed, because apparently the day was chosen not by the Pilgrims in Plymouth but rather for observance of the coronation of their Majesties William and Mary.

In 1941, Congress changed the date from the last Thursday to the third Thursday in November because sometimes it fell too close to Christmas.

But the idea for the day and its proclamation—that came from a lady from Newport, New Hampshire, named Sarah Josepha Hale. ❧

Aunt Jenny the Witch

MOST EVERY TOWN in New England has stories of witches, and the town of Hillsboro is no exception.

Hillsboro's Witch was a woman called Aunt Jenny Gilchrist.

Aunt Jenny lived out beside the Barden Hill Road back in the days when Hillsboro was called Old Number Seven.

The story goes that out at the North Branch of the Contoocook River there was a grist mill owned and operated by a man named (eponymously) John Miller. And Aunt Jenny and John Miller had an altercation about the price of his grain.

The upshot was that Aunt Jenny flew at the man and chased him across the surface of the mill pond. This was, it may be noted, not in the wintertime and running on water was an oddity.

Being unable to catch him she put a curse on his business and, sure enough, his health began to fail, and by fall the mill was out of business.

Another story is that Aunt Jenny ordered a passing child to gather up wood chips in a basket, and the child deferred saying she had not enough time to both pick up wood chips and get home before dark.

Aunt Jenny told her that if she picked up the chips she would see she got home in time. The child did the old woman's bidding and the witch waved her home. The little girl claimed that she sailed across the wood lots to her home with her feet never touching the ground.

They tried to put Aunt Jenny out of her home once, and a constable arrived at her door to conduct her on horseback to the alms house. He put her on the back of his saddle and rode all night only to find that the horse had gone in a circle and they were back at the old lady's home.

In the end Aunt Jenny died at home. She was then a very old lady.

She died, it is said, when a neighbor clubbed to death a sheep that had run mad.

When the neighbor hit the sheep, Aunt Jenny fell to the floor in convulsions.

They carried her to her bed and, it is said, on the stroke of midnight she departed this life.

She was called the Witch of Hillsboro.

Sanders McMurphy

THIS IS THE story of a young man from Alexandria, New Hampshire, by the name of Sanders Mc Murphy.

Sanders' dad, David, fought at Bennington with General Stark and was shot through the chest. Although he lived for many years he never fully recovered.

Sanders followed in his father's footsteps. He was six years in the Continental Army and even served with George Washington at Valley Forge.

This story about Sanders McMurphy was published some years ago in the *Bristol Enterprise*:

Seems on a November day at Valley Forge, General Washington was reviewing the troops when his eyes fell on young McMurphy. Of all the troops in the ranks that day, no one looked more wretched.

Washington approached the lad. "My brave boy," he said, "why are you so poorly clad? You have no shoes and your uniform is but rags."

"Because, sir," Sanders replied, "my country provides me with nothing better."

George Washington was deeply moved and gave young McMurphy a pass and instructed him to come to his headquarters that afternoon.

At three o'clock, the young soldier approached the general's compound where he presented the pass to the sentry. The sentry refused to let him in. The pass, he noted, must be forged.

This dismissal got the Scots-Irish temper of the young soldier up and an argument ensued which caught the attention of Martha Washington, the general's wife. (A note here: yes, George often had Martha in his quarters, even at Valley Forge.) Anyhow, Martha came out and directed the guard to let Sanders McMurphy pass. She then lead him to the general.

Now, I must note here that McMurphy was a tall man, as tall, in fact, as General Washington himself, which is why the general had called him here.

Before he left, Sanders McMurphy of Alexandria, New Hampshire, a common soldier, was outfitted in a uniform belonging to George Washington himself.

And for the next year, until he returned home to his farm, everyone called him "The Second Washington." ❧

The Minister's Pay

BACK IN COLONIAL times, the most important person in a community in New Hampshire was the settled minister.

In order to become a town, the citizens had to build a Meetinghouse and hire a preacher.

Of course, there was very little cash money back in those days and so the minister's salary was often payment-in-kind . . . that is, not money per se.

An example was found a few years back in the records of the town clerk in Northwood, New Hampshire. Here is a record of a vote taken on the 20th day of April in 1789. It concerns the hiring of a new preacher.

It says:

"Voted to have Mr. Elwood Pillsbury to preach for the whole parish for one year from the first of May next; one half of the time at the upper Meetinghouse and the other at the lower Meetinghouse.

"And that he have for support fifty bushel of corn, one hundred wait of beef. and to keep three cows, ten sheep, and one horse summer and winter. And fifty pounds of flax and five barrel of cider and twenty cord of wood hauled to his door.

"Which is the report of the committee as witness our hand."

The document is signed: Jona Clark, John Batchelder, Samuel Johnson, Sherbon Blake, and Henry Batchelder, committee.

Sounds like a pretty good deal to me. ◆

James Monroe Visits New Hampshire

LOTS OF PRESIDENTS have visited New Hampshire over the years. George Washington was the first. He came to New Hampshire during his first term.

President John Adams was familiar with Portsmouth and frankly, disliked the aristocracy there. Lincoln came to New Hampshire. So did Teddy Roosevelt. Woodrow Wilson had his summer White House over in Cornish. Grover Cleveland had a summer home in Tamworth.

But did you know that our fourth president, James Monroe, also visited the Granite State during his term? Well he did, in 1817. Came to Concord where he was wined and dined.

While in Concord, the president expressed a wish to visit Salisbury, New Hampshire. He thought it must be quite a town for it was the birthplace of Daniel Webster and also of Ichabod Bartlett. Both men had already made names for themselves in the U.S. House of Representatives. Little Salisbury was also the former home of U.S. Senator Thomas W. Thompson.

And so on Monday, the 21st of July, President Monroe and his entourage started north. The problem was, no one up there was expecting him. Actually, they had sent a man to Salisbury the day before so the president's arrival wouldn't be a complete shock. In Salisbury, a welcoming committee was formed that night to greet the president at the town's only hotel.

Sure enough, next day the president arrived. The chairman of the committee, a Mr. Greeley, came forward and said, "President Monroe, your visit to our rural town is so unexpected that we have had no time to give you such a reception as we would like to honor you with.

"I hope," he said, "you will take the will for the deed. Quite a number of our citizens have assembled at the tavern opposite, who are desirous of meeting you and grasping your hand."

Mr. Greeley went on to say that at four o'clock they had planned that the president would take the arm of Squire Bowers and stroll down the south side of the common to the Academy so that he might be seen by the citizens. Also, it would afford him an opportunity to meet the good men of the town and get a glimpse of the good women.

President Monroe, it is reported, replied that it would afford him "much pleasure to meet the good men," but that he wished "to get more than a glimpse of the good women." ●

Jonathan Moulton

JONATHAN MOULTON. THE name gives some people the willies.

He was a man of Colonial times who, it is said, sold his soul to the devil.

The amazing thing about this story is that there really was a Jonathan Moulton. The town of Moultonborough is named for him.

Jonathan Moulton came from Hampton. His home still stands. He was a colonel and later a general in the militia. He was a representative to the General Court from Hampton and later from Moultonborough.

And he was rich, made his money from what were called West Indian goods. West Indian Goods is a euphemism for rum and slaves. History tells us Colonel Moulton was always in court being sued by people he did business with. He was, most agree, not a completely honest man.

That may account for the legends that have grown up about him. There are two.

The first states that he was sitting by his fire one night when an elegant man appeared from the flames with a document for him to sign. For his soul the man would, once a month, fill the colonel's boots with gold coins. The colonel signed the agreement and for a year his boots were filled with gold as they hung by the fireplace.

But Jonathan Moulton was greedy and one night cut the soles from the boots so the gold fell into the room.

The devil, it is said, was so enraged that the house caught fire and burned to the ground. Moulton sifted the ashes for the melted coins but they had disappeared.

The second legend about Jonathan Moulton involves his wife with whom he had fifteen children. She died.

Before he buried her, Colonel Moulton removed her jewelry. This jewelry he gave to his next wife who awoke one night to feel a ghostly hand trying to remove her wedding ring.

This legend was the basis of John Greenleaf Whittier's poem, "A New Wife for the Old," where the first wife successfully takes back her jewelry to the grave. ✎

Ocean Born Mary

IN 1720, JAMES WILSON and his wife Elizabeth set sail from Northern Ireland, bound for New England and the new Scots-Irish settlement of Derry, New Hampshire. Elizabeth was over eight months pregnant.

On July 28, off the coast of Boston, the ship was overtaken by pirates and the crew and passengers taken captive.

During the takeover, Elizabeth gave birth. The pirate captain, hearing the sound of a baby, went to the cabin and asked if the child was a boy or a girl. When he learned it was a girl, he made a proposition. If the child was given the name of the pirate's mother, he would spare the lives of the crew and captives. Elizabeth Wilson consented.

And the pirate not only spared their lives. He also gave Elizabeth a bolt of light green silk brocade which was to be made into a wedding gown for Mary when she married.

And so it was that Ocean Born Mary got her name.

Yes, Ocean Born Mary was a real person.

And what we have said so far is true as far as we know. What isn't true about Ocean Born Mary is the legend that grew up around her.

But the true story is a great story. And this is it:

First of all, Mary's mother did get to Londonderry. But her father, James, did not. James died just after they docked in Boston.

When Elizabeth got to Londonderry, she married for a second time. Her new husband was James Clark, who was, incidentally, the great-great-grandfather of Horace Greeley.

So the years passed, and Ocean Born Mary grew into young womanhood. And, yes, she did marry and she did wear a gown of the pirate's silk at the ceremony.

She married, in fact, one James Wallace on December 18, 1742. A piece of the actual fabric of her gown is preserved in the Henniker Library.

Mary had grown, by the way, to be a tall, beautiful woman with shocking red hair and green eyes. All her life she spoke with a thick brogue and had a hearty laugh. Everyone, it seemed, loved her.

And, over the years, Ocean Born Mary gave birth to four sons and one daughter. Three of her sons married sisters, the daughters of Robert and Mary Moore of Londonderry. The three couples moved to Henniker where they built substantial homes.

So that is why Ocean Born Mary is buried in Henniker.

In her old age, when she was a widow, she came to live with her son William. She lived there sixteen years. She died February 13, 1814. She was 94.

It had been one heck of a life.

Oh, and the town of Londonderry for years, on her birthday, held an annual Day of Thanksgiving for the deliverance of Ocean Born Mary.

But what's all this about a legend? Well, here's that story:

Seems, back in 1917, a guy named Louis Roy from Wisconsin purchased the home that had been built by one of Mary's children, Robert. This was not the son she had lived with at the end of her life. That was William. But that didn't matter to Louis Roy.

Louis Roy, right off, claimed his house to be the one where Mary had died.

He invented a story about the pirate coming back to live with her in his old age and of burying gold in the apple orchard.

He said that Ocean Born Mary and the pirate captain were buried under the hearth of the fireplace, and that the captain, whom he called "Pedro," had the ship's carpenters build the house itself.

Why did Mr. Roy do this? Why, because he was charging admission to people to tour his house, and all this served to make people come.

They came to look for Mary's ghost, which Mr. Roy said he had seen many times. Louis Roy even rented spades for people to dig for buried gold in the orchard.

Books were written about the legend, even a prize-winning children's book; and many, if not most people, believed the false story. Most still do.

But, like I say, "It ain't true."

And about all the story has done, aside from making Louis Roy a living for awhile, is make a lot of nuisance for the people who now live in the old house which, even though it's not true, is still called, "The Ocean Born Mary House." ☙

Thomas Pickering Is Impressed

THE PICKERING FAMILY was one of the first families in Portsmouth.

Captain John Pickering had settled there in the 17th century. Captain John's son, Thomas, inherited the family farm on Great Bay in what is now Newington.

Not long after he had built a log home and had begun clearing land for the farm, a British man-o-war appeared in the harbor of the Piscataqua. They were looking to impress seamen, that is, forcibly take them to work on the ship. A press-gang, as it was called, rowed to the shore. They broke into segments of two men and went looking for victims.

Two men surprised Thomas Pickering at his work. They stopped and talked with him awhile and complimented him on his muscular appearance. "He was just such a man as his Majesty needed," they said. Then, with great importance, they commanded him to leave his work and follow them.

Thomas said that he was flattered but he had a young family who depended on him and he would have to decline.

"No excuse, sir," the officer said, "March!"

Well, Thomas then grabbed the officer by the back of his neck and threw him face down in the dirt. He then raised his ax as to cut off the man's head.

The man with the officer stayed his hand and begged for mercy.

Thomas let the man up and they scurried back to the ship.

Someone else would sail to England that day. ◆

The Road to the Cemetery

BACK IN MARCH of 1941, the citizens of Durham at their town meeting voted to surface the road between Doctor George G. McGregor's home and the Woodman Cemetery.

The doctor was outraged. A paved road only from his home to the cemetery! Was this a slur on his reputation!

Mrs. Oren V. Henderson discovered the unfortunate wording of the warrant article after the fact; that is, after the vote had been taken. Mrs. Henderson was the wife of a former executive councilor and so was conversant with article wording.

The wording was in fact, this:

"That the town would raise and appropriate the sum of seven hundred dollars to surface and tar Woodland Avenue from the residence of Dr. George G. McGregor to Woodman cemetery."

The article would have been less a slur had it not mentioned the doctor's residence.

The selectmen pointed out that there had been no slur intended to Dr. McGregor's reputation. They also noted that only six residents of Durham had died the year before and that the youngest of these was sixty-five.

Also, they noted that the cemetery had been abandoned and had not had a burial there in thirty years.

That being so, some folks wondered why they were improving the road out there.

The doctor, by the way, accepted the apology. No slur meant . . . none taken. ✎

Robert's Dad

AT WORK HE confided to a friend that his son, Robert, had applied to Harvard and had been turned down.

His friend had come from Exeter and suggested that Robert be sent to Phillips Exeter Academy, to prep. In a year, Robert could take the exam a second time. And so it was that Robert became a student at Phillips Exeter.

Six months passed and Robert's dad was invited to give a speech at a school in New York City. The speech was a great success. After the speech, Robert's dad took the train from New York up to Exeter to visit his son. The academy also invited him to give his speech a second time. And he accepted.

Robert had a room and he and his dad sat up a good part of the evening talking about his mom and the family and how he was doing in school and what a success his dad's speech had been. His dad then spent the night with his friend who had suggested the school in the first place. His friend had come back to town, in fact, to hear the speech.

The speech, given at the Exeter Town Hall, was as big a success as it had been when he gave it at the Cooper Union in New York City. In fact, before it was over, Robert's dad had the crowd on its feet cheering.

By now, no doubt, you have guessed who the other two players in this story were.

The time, by the way, was February of 1860.

The man from Exeter was Amos Tuck.

And Robert's dad was Amos Tuck's good friend and fellow congressman, Abraham Lincoln.

Robert, by the way, was accepted at Harvard the next year. ⤴

Count Rumford

FRANKLIN DELANO ROOSEVELT has written that, in his opinion, the three greatest American intellects of the 18th century were Ben Franklin, Thomas Jefferson and Benjamin Thompson.

And yet . . . the story of Benjamin Thompson is not taught in the public schools of the United States, and few people even in New Hampshire know much about him.

The reason, of course, is that during the American Revolution he was a Tory. Not only that, he was a Tory and a spy.

Now let me tell you about him.

First of all, Ben was born down in Woburn, Massachusetts, in 1753. His dad died before Ben turned two. The father had been a hard-scrabble farmer and very poor. Ben's mother remarried. The stepfather didn't have much use for the kid.

But a neighbor did. A guy named Loami Baldwin saw that this kid was special. He was very bright. And Loami taught him to read and to be intellectually curious; also, how to do scientific experiments. Ben especially loved doing things with fire and gunpowder.

Later Loami and Ben started a local society for the preservation of knowledge and useful information . . . a school.

Now, when Ben was only 19, he met the Reverend Timothy Walker, who was the settled minister in Concord, New Hampshire (which, back then, was a part of Massachusetts called Rumford). The Reverend told him the town needed a school and asked him to come up and found one.

So Ben came along and, what do you know? The Reverend Tim had a daughter, Sarah. Sarah was older than Ben (she was 30 . . . and he, as I say, was 19). Sarah had been married to another guy named Benjamin . . . old Benjamin Rolfe. I say old because he was double Sarah's age when they married, and he died just two years later, leaving her with a newborn son.

Old Ben Rolfe had been the most prosperous person in Concord. So the widow was rich. Ben Thompson was tall and thin and blue eyed. In his youth he looked like Richard Chamberlain. Sarah didn't have a chance. She was smitten. She and Ben were married, and Ben moved into the mansion, now the richest man in town.

Sally was soon pregnant again.

All this money made him important and soon he was hobnobbing with none other than John Wentworth, the royal governor. Here's another guy who looked like a movie star. Together they were a synergy.

Soon a daughter was born to Ben and Sarah. They named her after her mother, but they called her "Sally." The same week Sally was born, Governor John Wentworth made Ben Thompson a major in New Hampshire's "15th Royalist Regiment."

That really teed off a lot of the members of the regiment who were mostly veterans of the French and Indian Wars, and the fact that a 21-year-old dandy was their superior did not sit well.

But Ben used his position to ingratiate himself with the high brass of the British military in America and, specifically, with the biggest cheese of all, General Thomas Gage, the British Army's number one man here, and later with General William Howe, his successor.

In fact, Ben Thompson was sending the generals regular reports about the Continental Army and their strengths, and who was plotting, and what the political situation was here. He wrote these messages in invisible ink.

Ben was a spy.

In Concord, they had enough finally, and they were going to tar and feather him. But Ben Thompson escaped to Boston and thence to London, leaving his wife and daughter to fend for themselves in the Rolfe mansion.

Ben arrived in London bearing a letter of introduction to Lord George Germain from General Howe. Lord George was the secretary of the colonies. It was he that had made most of the mess in America.

Lord George was impressed with Ben. In fact, he made him undersecretary for the Colonies. In this position, Ben provided men and materials for the war. Along with his title, he got lots of kickbacks and was able to steal a lot more. Soon he was very, very rich, indeed.

Now this was "The Age of Enlightenment," and London was gaga over science. Soon Ben met Samuel Johnson, Edmund Burke, Adam Smith . . . and also Sir Joseph Banks, the president of The Royal Society.

One day he and Sir Joseph were discussing whether cannon balls traveled further when shot in wet weather. It was generally thought that gunpowder burned with a better consistency in wet weather and so the balls traveled better.

Ben set up an experiment (you remember he had experimented with gunpowder as a lad in Waltham). He shot a cannon over 120 times with various charges and amounts of misted water.

The result was unequivocal: Gunpowder worked best dry and on dry days.

For this work, Ben was made a member of The Royal Society, and from then on he signed his name with the addendum, FRS (Fellow of the Royal Society).

Then in 1782, Ben Thompson came back to America and headed up a band of guerrillas around Yorktown. He did a lot of mischief with his group of dragoons made up of Tories and mercenaries.

The Brits lost, but Ben's bunch got great press back home and back in England. George III himself awarded Ben Thompson the rank of colonel and gave him half pay for life. Ben Thompson was only 30 years old.

He hung around London for a few months . . . but his experience in Yorktown had gone to his head. He wanted to be in a war. The Austrians and the Ottoman Turks were fighting, and so Ben boarded a ship bound for The Continent. On board he met the historian Edward Gibbon who wrote in his diary, "Met Mr. Secretary, Colonel, Admiral, Philosopher Thompson. . . ."

On this trip Ben Thompson also met the nephew of the Elector of Bavaria. The nephew was impressed and gave a letter of introduction to his uncle, one Karl Theodore.

To make a long story short, Ben never got to Austria where he was heading. Instead, he managed to snow Herr Theodore. He told him he could fix the army and make Bavaria the showplace of the world. Theodore promptly offered him a position in his government.

Ben, however, needed the permission of the English King to accept a position with a foreign government. After a lot of correspondence over a year, George III agreed to let him do it . . . provided . . . he would spy for the English Crown.

Ben agreed and for this he was knighted. From then on, he was "Sir" Benjamin.

For the next 16 years, Sir Benjamin lived in Munich. He had affairs and made friends. He learned to speak German. He fathered a daughter with his mistress. They named the child, "Sophie."

He established a laboratory, and he studied the army and the social conditions of the country.

And he reached conclusions which he delivered to his benefactor.

Briefly, what he said was this: "The Bavarian aristocracy, military caste, and civil administration are steeped in a morass of decadence, indolence and corruption. The army robs and torments the peasants and the officers are sadistic and cruel to the lower ranks. Something needs to be done."

For an answer, the Elector of Bavaria awarded Ben Thompson the title of Minister of War and gave him full discretionary power to fix things.

Sir Ben started by firing 800 officers of the army. He then established permanent garrisons for the troops which were near to their families. He built roads and schools and put in a method of farming which the men did when not at war. The army also built dams and drained swamps when not soldiering. In other words, Sir Ben established the first public works administration in history.

And a lot of what the soldiers grew were potatoes. See, Sir Ben had become aware of the potato and found it nutritious and easy to grow, and it could be kept for long times. Under his guidance the army diet was based on the potato. He even invented a soup which is sold to this day in Munich and bears his name.

And he began the construction of the largest public park in the world in Munich, over 900 acres. It was called the Englicsher Garten after Sir Ben. It was built entirely by the Bavarian Army and at first was for their use alone. There was a parade ground and a veterinary hospital and barracks.

But this was the time of the French Revolution. In Paris, they were using the guillotine, and all over Europe the people of the aristocracy were scared to death.

Sir Ben advised the Elector that a grand gesture would be to present this park to the people for their general use. This would, he thought, be a vaccination against what was called the "French Infection."

Did it work?

You bet! The park was wildly popular and a couple years later, when Sir Ben took sick, the citizens of the city turned out in the park to pray for him, and when he recovered six months later, some 30,000 people turned out to celebrate his recovery.

Next, he reformed the prisons in Bavaria with humane treatment for the inmates and health services and education.

One day he rounded up all the beggars in Munich . . . some 2,600 people . . . and relocated them in abandoned factories where they were given food and shelter, medical treatment, clean clothes, and a place to work. The crafts turned out by the inmates there made the place self-sufficient.

Sir Ben's famous quote is: "To make a vicious and abandoned people happy, it was thought that first they had to be made virtuous. I say, why not make them happy first and then virtuous?"

Also during this time, Sir Ben continued his laboratory experimentation.

He developed an accurate photometer and a candle so consistent in its light that it was used as a measure . . . for foot candles.

In 1792, Karl Theodore made Sir Benjamin Thompson a Bavarian Peer. He could, the Elector said, choose any name he wished. Benjamin Thompson chose the name Concord had, when it was part of Massachusetts and was ruled by Britain. He chose Count von Rumford, the Count of Rumford.

That very month of 1792, his wife Sarah died in Concord. They had not seen each other since he had hightailed it to London in 1776.

You must be wondering about Sally.

Well, after her dad skidaddled, Sally was sent to live with her grandmother in Waltham where she grew up.

And now that his wife was dead, Count Rumford began writing his daughter.

In 1795, he went back to London for a visit.

Soon he had reestablished his place in London society and had a mistress, Lady Palmerston. And it is Lady Palmerston's bedroom that is responsible for the one thing most everyone knows about Count Rumford.

Seems they were in the room one night when the fireplace caught a downdraft and filled the room with smoke.

"This will not do," the Count said, and promptly had workmen come and build a fireplace to the his specifications. It was shallow so as to radiate heat into the room. There was a narrow throat with what he called a smoke shelf, which created a venturi . . . that is, the air pressure above the shelf was less than below, and it sucked the smoke out of the room.

Soon nearly every chimney fireplace in the world was built that way and, to this day, the design is call the Rumford Fireplace.

By the way, he said at the time that he had gotten the idea from Ben Franklin.

While he was in London, Sally arrived from Waltham and Concord. She was 21 years old, and a disappointment.

She was uneducated (and whose fault was that?) and loud and not refined. She curtsied to the servants! The Count barely tolerated her and he drove all her suitors off. The result was that in the end she died a spinster.

About this time, Austria and France were at war at the doorstep of Munich. Karl Theodore wanted the Count back. He and Sally arrived in the nick of time. Both armies were at the gates, and the Elector and his family were fleeing the city.

Before he left, Karl Theodore bestowed Count Rumford with the title "Commander and Chief of Bavaria." That, in effect, made him the dictator and most powerful man in the country.

Both armies made it known to him that should he favor their enemy they would sack the city. It took four days, but in the end, France withdrew and Austria and Munich were saved.

And Count Rumford had another title, "Commander and Chief," like our president.

The Elector returned and sent Count Rumford back to England . . . this time as the official ambassador of the country. But London would not accept his credentials because he was an English citizen, and he could not represent a foreign government.

Nonetheless, with Sir Joseph Bales, Count Rumford then founded The Royal Institute of Great Britain, which he ran for the first two years.

But Count Rumford's imperious ways were not to the liking of the academics there at the institute and he finally resigned.

He and Sally then went off to Paris where he was wined and dined and elected to the French Academy, the only American, other than Thomas Jefferson, to be so honored.

Here again, he made scientific history by proving that heat was not a substance. It seems silly nowadays, but even a scientist as important as Antoin Lavoisier had proclaimed heat a substance.

Count Rumford's experiment was simplicity itself. He drilled a hole in a piece of metal submerged in water, and the heat generated from the drilling boiled the water.

And speaking of Lavoisier, Lavoisier's widow, Marie, and the Count met at a soiree one afternoon and within a month were married. He loved her the first year . . . tolerated her the second . . . argued with her the third (she, on one occasion, poured boiling water on his growing flowers) . . . and divorced her the fourth year.

In 1810, he settled down in France with his housekeeper, Victoria LeFeve, with whom he fathered a son, Charles.

Sally stayed in Paris and later went to London to live. In the summer of 1814, Count Rumford took sick with a fever and within a week was dead.

He is buried in France. His tombstone mentions his Bavarian and French titles and accomplishments, but makes no mention of either England or America.

When she was 71, Sally, that is, Sarah, the Countess Rumford, returned to Concord. She lived another ten years in the house where she was born. She left most of her money to charity, including a large bequest to the Concord State Mental Hospital.

And that's the story of Benjamin Thompson, Sir Benjamin, Count Rumford, Fellow of the Royal Society, Member of the French Academy, soldier, social reformer, scientist, commander and chief, and inventor of thousands of practical things that we did not mention.

Things like the pressure cooker, the turbo oven, the coffee maker, the kitchen range.

He was a cad and a genius, a snob and a hero of the common people, a spy and a patriot. An amazing man.

The largest park in Munich is his work. The finest avenue in the city, Maximillian Strasse, has a huge statue of the Count. There is even a Rumford Strasse . . . and, of course, Rumford "Soupe."

But Concord, New Hampshire, has very little about the man. About all we have is a printing company and a baking soda brand named for him.

This place may have forgotten him, but we know, because of the name he chose, he never forgot this place. ✒

The Russian Count in Meredith

YOU HAVE HEARD the story about a man named Benjamin Thompson who, just at the start of the American Revolution, left what is now Concord and went out to the greater world and became an Austrian count. He took the name Count Rumford.

But did you know there was a man from Meredith, New Hampshire, who also went out to the greater world and also became a count? The man's name was Peter Williams. He was the son of the local pastor, Rev. Simon Finley Williams.

Young Pete was bound out by his father to a merchant in what was then Meredith Bridge and is now Laconia. This was about 1796 and Peter was 17 years old.

One night the lad went out to see some young ladies and came in very late.

His employer the next morning whipped him with, the history tells us, "twigs from the wilderness."

This did not suit the son of a preacher, and the next evening Peter Williams stole $300 from his employer's desk and hightailed it on foot over to Ossipee. There he hired a man to take him to Portland.

In the meantime, the police from Meredith were hot on his trail. Peter Williams just barely got aboard a Russian merchant ship which sailed two hours before the police arrived.

On the passage to Russia, the ship was attacked by two pirate ships. Young Peter convinced the captain not to surrender. Instead, he and two other seamen manned a cannon and with it they managed to sink both ships just as they came abreast of the Russian ship.

When they arrived in St. Petersburg, news of the battle reached the emperor. He summoned the young boy and rewarded him. In time, Peter Williams became admiral-in-chief of the entire Russian navy.

In 1831, Peter Williams returned to America. He came from Boston to Meredith in a coach and four, and found his former employer was still alive.

He knocked on his door. The old man appeared.

"I am Count Zinchercoff of St. Petersburg," he said.

"I do not know you, sir," the old man said.

"Do you remember a boy named Williams you gave a thrashing to some years ago and who stole $300 from your desk? Well, I am that boy," the count said, "and I have come from Russia to pay the bill. How much is it?"

The old man said he would be satisfied with the amount taken and the count paid him back in gold coins . . . with interest.

"I go back to Russia an honest man," he said, and turned and rode away, never to be seen in America again. ✎

Harlan Fiske Stone

HE WAS BORN in Chesterfield, on a farm, in the height of the foliage color, October 11, 1872.

He hated the farm. But he did his chores and grew strong and athletic. He was one of those naturally smart kids and he loved to read. And he knew scholarship would save him.

But it almost did not. In fact, because of his vocation, his family sent him to the Massachusetts Agricultural College where he got into hijinx and curfew problems and was expelled.

But his next stop was Amherst College, where he was a fine athlete and a great baseball player. And he got straight A's . . . graduated Phi Beta Kappa in 1894.

In 1895, he was a "master" at Newburgh, New York, High School. The next year, he taught history at Adelphi Academy in Brooklyn. But then he entered law school at Columbia University. He was the best of his class, and upon graduation he was immediately hired by the school as a professor. Along with teaching, he was a partner in the prestigious firm of Sullivan and Cromwell. He got rich.

Then President Warren Harding had a heart attack in office. Calvin Coolidge became president. "Silent" Cal was an old friend and fellow Republican. Coolidge named him his attorney general and the next year nominated him to the Supreme Court.

I guess, by now, you have figured out who we are talking about.

The man is Justice Harlan Fiske Stone.

Stone was to serve on the Supreme Court for the next 21 years. In 1941, Franklin Delano Roosevelt elevated Harlan Stone to chief justice. He had served only five years when he died in 1946.

What kind of justice was Harlan Stone?

Well, for a Republican, he was quite liberal. He fought FDR when he tried to increase the size of the court and appoint his own guys. Still, between 1937 and 1941, Roosevelt managed to put a liberal majority on the bench. As a relatively liberal Republican, Stone was the perfect political appointment.

But he was not a noted justice. And, as chief justice, he was not good at keeping order on the court where it seemed all the members hated one another. Harlan Fiske Stone is, in fact, remembered in law school textbooks for a footnote he wrote to a case regarding government economic legislation.

The footnote is to a case entitled *U.S. v. Carolene Products.* It is referred to as simply, "Footnote Four," and what it says is that in non-economic legislation, the court must have a higher level of scrutiny to protect rights of gender, race and religion. That standard is maintained to this day by the court. Harlan Fiske Stone is Chesterfield, New Hampshire's, most famous citizen. ✎

Last Signer

WHO WAS THE first signer of the Declaration of Independence?

Easy. John Hancock. It was the biggest signature, too. He wanted George the Third to see it.

No doubt, the best-known autograph in America.

So you get stars for that answer. Now a harder question: Who was the last to sign the Declaration of Independence? Whose is the last signature on the page?

Want a hint. OK, this guy has an insurance company named after him. No, it is not John Hancock again, even though Johnnie would have loved to have signed twice.

Now, think it out. This segment is called, "Fritz Wetherbee's New Hampshire" so it has to be a signer from the Granite State. That leaves us with Josiah Bartlett, William Whipple and Matthew Thornton Health Care. Oops, I told you, didn't I?

Anyhow you were ahead of me.

But here's another: Do you know why Matthew Thornton was the last to sign?

It had to do with his foot. See, Matt had gout. Horrible stuff, gout. Couldn't stand on his foot. Couldn't walk.

So when the guys got together on the Fourth of July down in Independence Hall in Philadelphia and put their John Hancocks on the Declaration, Matt couldn't be there. Too painful a trip.

But then King George learned of the Declaration, and he had a fit. This was serious. This would lead to war if unchecked.

And so King Georgie got together with his ministers and drew up a document which said in effect, that if the Colonists would eschew the Declaration, he, George the Third, would also make concessions.

He would repeal the Stamp Act. He would allow America a certain amount of representation in the English Government, and he would lower taxes over here in general.

All we, over here, had to do was agree to go along with him. And also we had to turn over the actual signers of the document so the Brits could hang them.

Well, Matthew Thornton had not signed the Declaration. If it came down to it, he would never be hanged.

That was intolerable.

And so he hitched up his horse to his carriage here in Londonderry, put his throbbing foot up on the dash of the vehicle, and drove all the way to Philadelphia, where he guaranteed his demise should the venture fail.

Last signer.

Pretty neat story, don't you think? ⚓

The Tramp

IN ASHLAND THERE is a rise of land called "Christian Hill." But that was not always the name of the place.

In the early days of Ashland it was called "Indian Hill." But when they put a cemetery up there, it got the new name. The town history says that there are two theories about how the name came about.

One theory is that it was because Rueben Whitten lived up there, and he was regarded as a good Christian gentleman.

The other theory was that, because the road to the top was so steep and sandy, anyone who could climb the hill without cursing was a good Christian.

Another cemetery story told in the *Ashland Town History* concerns the Samuel Baker family, who lived in the Preuss home on Thompson Street.

The story goes that on an extremely cold November night in 1890 a tramp showed up at the Baker home asking for something warm to drink.

Mr. Baker gave the tramp a hot cup of tea and a hot bowl of soup and set a cot up out in the summer kitchen of the house. Back then many people had a second kitchen, usually out in a rear shed in a place with cross ventilation because it got so hot in the summertime in the inside kitchen.

In this case, Mr. Baker set a fire in the stove out there and allowed the tramp to sleep warm by the fire.

In the middle of the night he got up to put more wood in the stove and check on his guest. He found the poor man dead.

The tramp's pockets contained nothing to denote who he was and so Sam Baker made a simple pine-box coffin for him and the visitor was buried in the Mooney Cemetery where he resides to this day, unknown but, at least at the end, respected. ◦

Amos Tuck

ON THE CORNER of Front and Court streets, within sight of downtown Exeter, is a large brick building known as "A.P. Blake's Hotel." It may be among the most important places in America, for it was there that history was made back in 1853.

See, this was a time when the slavery issue was the most important issue in the country. The Democrats and the Whigs controlled politics. Franklin Pierce had just been elected president as a Democrat. It was the same election in which John Parker Hale of Dover had been expelled from the party for his radical views, and principally because he refused to support the annexation of Texas as a slave state. Hale had reacted by running for president as a "Free Soiler" against Pierce. He lost big time. But standing with John Hale was a U.S. Congressman from Exeter, a man named Amos Tuck.

Tuck was close friends with another rebel congressman, Abraham Lincoln. Because of the slave issue, new political parties were popping up left and right . . . "Independent" . . . "Free Soil" . . . a party called the "Democratic Republicans," and the Whig Party was wasting away.

The problem was that there was no single banner under which the reformers could gather. That is, until Congressman Tuck called a meeting of all the disparate parties in the state. They came and met in a room in Exeter. And there they decided to join together under a single name and that name was "Republican." Yes, that is the very spot where the Republican Party was born.

Horace Greeley—who was born in Amherst, New Hampshire, and was the publisher of the *New York Tribune*—gave the new party the publicity it needed to take root.

Incidentally, Tuck and Greeley and Lincoln were once all congressmen at the same time. They knew and liked each other and, perhaps more importantly, they agreed on issues.

Later on, members of the Republican Party were to claim that it was formed in Rippon, Wisconsin. The problem with that assertion is this: That meeting was held a year later, and the official history of the party was written by a Rippon College professor. Former New

Hampshire Governor Hugh Gregg, along with his co-author, Georgi Hippauf, have researched all claims and their conclusion is unequivocal: The Republican Party had its birth in that building in Exeter, New Hampshire, in 1853. ❧

Mark Twain in Dublin

IN THE LATE 19th and early 20th centuries, because of the railroads, it became fashionable to estivate ... that is, to leave the sweltering cities in the summer and come to stay in a more temperate place.

In July, the gentry would pack up and move for the entire summer to hotels on the Maine seacoast or in the New Hampshire mountains. They also came to hotels in places nearer to Boston, such as Jaffrey or Mont Vernon where the elevation made nights cooler. There was a lot of expendable income back before the income tax and many wealthy people built more permanent summer homes.

Dublin, New Hampshire, was one of those places where the wealthy came to estivate.

The Dublin Colony, as it was called, soon developed a reputation for attracting artists and art patrons.

The painter, George de Forest Brush came to Dublin, as did the noted Harvard Egyptologist Joseph Linden Smith, who had a home there. Secretary of the Treasury Franklin MacVeagh summered in Dublin ... even President William Howard Taft spent time there.

But, probably, as noted a visitor as Dublin ever had was Samuel Langhorne Clements ... that is, Mark Twain.

How, you may wonder, did the chronicler of Tom Sawyer and Huck Finn ... of life on the Mississippi ... find his way to Dublin?

Well, the answer is that, although Mark Twain lived the first half of his life in Missouri and New Orleans and points south, in 1870, when he was thirty-five, he married one Olivia Langdon. She had him settle down to a respectable life in Hartford, Connecticut. Twain loved her as he loved his two daughters ... and he outlived them all.

The latter part of his life was a struggle. He was always in money trouble. He was no businessman. Seems all his investments went sour. In his old age, he was forced to lecture ... to give humorous talks ... in order to pay his creditors.

In 1904, Mark Twain's wife died and he found himself rattling around alone in the big gingerbread house in Hartford. One of his daughters had been to Dublin and she suggested he rent a house there for the summer.

He found a lovely place up on a small hill where he could see across the lake. From there, he could look one way to Mt. Monadnock and the other way over Dublin Lake.

I have personally talked with people who remembered the white-haired gentleman with the white suit and black armband who came to town for his mail and was pleasant to everyone. He wrote that year that it was as restful and beautiful a summer as he had ever had.

The next year he came again to Dublin, but the house he had rented the summer before was not available and he spent some weeks at another house over on Jaffrey Road.

But the experience was not as good and he never came again.

Both of Mark Twain's daughters died within the next two years. He himself lived another five years. He died in 1910. ❧

The Snowball Fight

BACK IN THE early 1800s, a young man named Jesse Billings came to be the schoolmaster in a one-room schoolhouse in Sanbornton.

Mr. Billings was a Dartmouth man. Class of 1808. He knew his stuff but he was not a disciplinarian.

That winter there was a great deal of snow.

Now one afternoon the kids were out in the schoolyard when a snowball fight broke out, and the older boys pelted their foes with such energy that one of the boys, a kid named James Severance, fell to the ground in great pain.

Turned out poor James had caught one of the snowballs in his side. The snowball was of inordinate size and maybe had an ice core. Whatever it was, the poor young man suffered a couple broken ribs.

Well, things seemed fine until young James went home. There he was unable to do his chores . . . milking and tending the hens and cutting and carrying wood. And James' dad was livid and he, the dad in high dudgeon, paid a visit to Schoolmaster Billings.

What was to be done?

Well, Schoolmaster Billings called a trial there at the schoolhouse. The judge was Mr. Billings and some of the kids were the jury.

The trial lasted the entire afternoon and most of the kids involved in the melee gave testimony. No one was singled out for punishment as the verdict was that there had been no direct malice but rather an over-exuberance in the prosecution of the snowball fight.

That being said, the court was not unaware of the family problems caused by the broken ribs, and young James Severance was awarded by the court, a lamb.

The town history tells us that everyone seemed quite pleased with the verdict. ♣

Wadleigh School

FOR OVER A hundred years, on West 114 Street in New York City, right in the middle of Harlem, a great pile of Victorian brick has dominated the neighborhood. It is a high shool. It is, in fact, the oldest high school in Harlem.

Now you may wonder what a graveyard in North Sutton, New Hampshire, has to do with a public high school in Harlem.

The reason: That school in Harlem is named for the lady who is buried there. It is the grave of Lydia Wadleigh, and the school in Harlem is the Wadleigh Secondary School.

Go figure. And, in fact, that's just what we are going to do, "go figure." That is, find out the story.

So, who was Lydia Wadleigh?

She was the daughter of Judge Benjamin Wadleigh, who lived in North Sutton back in the beginning of the 19th century. Lydia was born in 1817. She was the youngest child.

Judge Wadleigh was a progressive thinker and saw that his daughters were as well educated as his sons.

And Lydia had a talent for learning. At first she attended School House Number Seven in North Sutton. From there she went to the New Hampton Literary and Scientific Institution in New Hampton, New Hampshire.

She graduated with honors and was offered a teaching position there, which she accepted. She was a very good teacher, although a strict disciplinarian.

Over the years, word of this exceptional woman spread, and she rose quickly in the ranks of education. She taught at Miss Ellis' school in Hanover; she was the lady principal at the ladies' academy in Derry. She taught at Georgetown in Washington, D.C., and in Philadelphia, and in Freehold, New Jersey.

By the way, her teaching specialties were Greek, mathematics and English literature.

In the 1850s, there were no public high schools for girls in New York City and a lot of people there thought this was wrong. At the time, it was thought by many that educating women was a waste of time.

But the Department of Education in New York City decided to do an experiment. It would create one high school in the city which would be open solely to young women.

And, because of her stellar reputation, they offered the position of principal of this experimental school to, you guessed it, Lydia Wadleigh.

The school opened in an older building on East Twelfth Street, a building that had housed a grammar school.

The Twelfth Street School was not a favorite of the establishment in the city. From the start there were not enough textbooks. Lydia herself and her teaching staff paid for the textbooks themselves out of their salaries.

The school was, of course, a huge success. In 1859, eleven young women graduated. They were the first female high school graduates from a public school in the history of the city. The success was attributed to Lydia's vision and perseverance.

Its success spawned the first teachers' college in the city, the New York Normal School. Lydia was a full professor at the school and its vice president. This school went on to become Hunter College.

By now, Lydia Wadleigh was the highest-paid woman teacher in New York State. The high school she founded was then named after her, the Wadleigh Secondary School.

In 1888, Lydia Wadleigh died on a trip to Paris. Her body was returned and buried in the place where she was born.

A dozen years later, the school she founded was moved to a new building in Harlem. For some years it remained strictly a girls' school, but today it is co-educational.

Among its graduates are writer Lillian Hellman and actress Jean Stapleton. ✒

Daniel Minds His Manners

THE PLACE WHERE Daniel Webster learned table manners is the Gillman/Clifford Garrison house in Exeter.

It was built in 1690 as protection from the Indians for the local sawmills. Parts of the interior of this house contain the stacked logs used in the original construction. There was also a thick wooden portcullis that could be dropped in front of the door should there be an attack.

Later on, this house was added onto and brought up to the standards of the mid-18th century.

It was in this building that Governor John Wentworth met with his favorite Colonial battalion, whom he called his "Cadets." The governor spent a lot of his money on the very best uniforms, weapons, and training of his men. However, when the Revolutionary War came along, Wentworth's Cadets went off to fight for the American side. So much for loyalty.

John Phillips was a colonel in Wentworth's Cadets. Phillips went on to found Phillips Exeter Academy.

This building today is owned by the Society for the Preservation of New England Antiquities. Now for the story of Daniel Webster acquiring good manners in this house.

Seems Webster was a student at the Academy at the time, about 1796, and he boarded there with the owner, one Ebeneezer Clifford.

Ebeneezer and his wife were appalled at the young Webster's table manners. He slurped and smacked and ate with his knife. It was terrible. See, Daniel Webster had grown up in the woods of what was then Salisbury, New Hampshire. There was little society in Salisbury, and no one to provide any example of how to behave in genteel company.

The Cliffords were not truly genteel company but they were townspeople and knew what was and what was not rude behavior. They also noted that young Daniel was a brilliant student and, more to the point, sensitive. They liked him a great deal and did not wish to hurt his feelings.

Ebeneezer Clifford was a woodworker and employed a young

apprentice in his shop, and it was through this apprentice that they solved the problem.

Seems it was okay for Ebeneezer to correct the manners and etiquette of his worker who, in the custom of the time, ate at the same table.

So Ebeneezer would scold his apprentice for the same faults he observed in Daniel Webster. He was relieved to note that the quick-witted young student needed no more and soon became as conversant with gentility as any young man in the town. ✒

Doctor Whipple

OF ALL THE people who have lived in the town of Ashland over the years, the most noted is, no doubt, Dr. George Hoyt Whipple.

Dr. Whipple's father himself was an M.D. who practiced in Ashland in the mid-1800s. His son, George, was born in August of 1878. George's middle name, Hoyte, was his mother Frances' maiden name.

Young George was a very bright student. For secondary school he went to Phillips Andover and Yale and later studied medicine at Johns Hopkins. He became an M.D. like his dad in 1905. But, unlike his dad, Dr. George devoted his career to research. And he was good at it.

Other researchers depended on their young assistant and, by the age of 36, he was the director of the Hooper Foundation for Medical Research at the University of California. By the age of 42, he was the dean of the medical school there.

His field was anaemia caused by parasites. His interest in this field came from a stint he took in Panama right after graduating from med school. Later, he was the one to discover that cells in the liver have an almost limitless power of regeneration.

And he discovered revolutionary ways of treating pernicious anaemia and for this work he, along with his colleagues, George Minot and William Murphy, won the Nobel Prize for Medicine in 1934.

Dr. George Hoyt Whipple died on the first of February, 1976, at the age of 98.

Six years earlier he had bequeathed the Whipple family home to the town of Ashland to be used as a museum. The town accepted, making two historical museums in this small town . . . the other being the old train depot which the Ashland Historical Society restored in 1997. This building, along with other historical artifacts, also contains the Pauline E. Gidden Toy Museum. ❧

Prince Whipple

BACK IN COLONIAL times, one of the most-noted, respected, and beloved members of the Portsmouth community was an African American, who was called Prince Whipple.

The man's name, according to author Charles Brewster, came because his father had been a king on the West African coast. The king, according to the story, sent his ten-year-old son to America for an education. Times being what they were, the sea captain who transported the lad took the father's money and promptly sold the boy into slavery.

That's Charles Brewster's story. Whether it is true or not cannot be proved.

But Prince Whipple certainly was a handsome man, tall and regal. He grew up as the slave to one of New Hampshire's signers of the Declaration of Independence, Captain William Whipple. As with many slaves, he was given the last name of his owner.

Portsmouth, at the time of the Revolution, had a large and thriving black community, and Prince Whipple became the most important person in that community.

Now, William Whipple was wealthy and highly respected in Portsmouth and was a driving force in New Hampshire's first independent government. When it came to sending men to the war, the council chose two men for the command of two brigades. William Whipple was given command of the First Brigade and John Stark, the Second Brigade. Both men were given the rank of "Brigadier General."

Stark went off, of course, to trounce Burgoyne at the Battle of Bennington and change the course of the war. But Whipple and his First Brigade, too, went down in the history books for their fierce fighting in the battle at Saratoga under General Gates. It was there that Burgoyne surrendered.

William Whipple returned a hero. But his attendant and aide at the battle, Prince Whipple, returned with even more pride.

The story is that, as the two men left Portsmouth for the battle-front, Prince was sulky and in ill humor. General Whipple upbraided his slave.

Brewster tells us that Prince replied, "Master, you are going to fight for your liberty, but I have none to fight for."

General Whipple is said to have replied, "Do your duty and from this hour you will be free."

And so it was that the former black slave, Prince Whipple, returned to Portsmouth from the Revolutionary War, a hero . . . and, more importantly, a free man.

So there you have it.

Except for one other thing. In the famous painting, "George Washington Crossing the Delaware," you will note a dark face just in front of and to the right of the Father of Our Country. The man depicted is manning an oar and guiding the craft through the ice.

Next time you see the picture, look closely, for that is the face of Prince Whipple. ✎

Israel Woodbury

THIS IS A story told by Levi Woodbury in the *Salem Town History*. It is a story about his grandfather.

His grandfather's name was Israel . . . Israel Woodbury.

The story begins just after the Battle of Bunker Hill. It was at this time that Israel Woodbury went off to fight for his country. He was seventeen years old, and his parents were not pleased that he left. And this was not just because they loved him. It was a hard life in the late 1700s, and his folks needed him on the farm.

Nevertheless, they let him go. One reason was that the family had adopted another boy who was just Israel's age . . . a boy named Amos. Because Amos would continue working on the farm, Israel was allowed to go.

The young man was sent to a fort in northern New York. As soon as he arrived, a measles epidemic infected the entire company. Men were dying all around him. Those who recovered were sent immediately into battle.

Israel himself succumbed to the disease. He was near death when the fort was overrun by marauding Indians. Anyone who tried to escape was killed. Israel was too weak to resist and, as a result, was carried off to the St. Lawrence River, where he was turned over to the family of a French officer to be kept in servitude.

Years passed. Israel was not even allowed to write a letter to his parents. Back home they gave him up for dead.

Seven years went by. One day the young man saw his chance and escaped. For weeks he walked south from Canada, and on a spring day he arrived on his parents' doorstep. It was Sunday and his folks were attending church.

Amos answered the door and upon seeing Israel, he began to scream.

"Israel's ghost!" he hollered, "Israel's ghost!" Amos then ran into the house to hide.

But Israel said, "Amos," he said, "Amos, ghosts do not carry guns."

And then, according to Levi Woodbury's story, there was such hand shaking and embracing between such friends as was never seen before.

Then Israel's parents came up the road both riding on the same horse; the father, on the saddle, and his wife on a pillion at the rear.

Amos bounded out of the house. "Israel has come!" he shouted. "Israel has come!"

Well, Amos was known to be a jokester, and the Woodburys were not amused. They had, in fact, just been praying for the soul of their dead son. So the father whopped at Amos with the horse whip, and Amos yelped and ran inside. He appeared once again in the door. "See his gun!" he shouted.

And just then Israel himself appeared at the door. His mother jumped from the horse and embraced him and so did his father.

In fact, the *Salem Town History* tells us, there was rejoicing in the entire town. ✎

THE WETHERBEES

The Grand Hotel

A STEEL ENGRAVING used to hang in my grandfather's dentist office. It always fascinated me.

The subject was the old Grand Hotel in Mont Vernon. My grandfather and grandmother used to go there a lot. At the turn of the 20th century, it was the fanciest and most exciting place around.

The Grand Hotel was completed in 1891. That year my grandfather was 28 years old. The hotel was built atop Prospect Hill and, back then, there were very few trees in the region. As a result, you could see all the way to Boston from the two-story cupola lookout atop the structure.

The hotel was built of wood. It was a hundred feet wide and a hundred feet long. There was a veranda all around it and two great stairways that lead up to the veranda.

Inside was a huge lobby, 37 by 37 feet, which opened 75 feet to the roof of the building. From there light poured down from the windows on all four sides.

Inside the main structure, four stories circled the lobby with tiered balconies on each floor. Every room opened onto the inside space, and every room had a spectacular view.

Off the lobby were an office, a drawing room and a dining room. Each had a huge fieldstone fireplace. The lobby had potted plants and the parlor was a riot of hollyhocks.

Outside there was a swimming pool with two waterslides, one

simple slide and another which had a water toboggan. There was a golf course and a baseball field, a croquet lawn and tennis courts. Around a stand of birches there was a raised tree-house promenade with a telescope where one could see Boston or the mountains or who was cheating on the golf course.

Inside there were card tables, pool tables, a bowling alley and a piano. During meals, a violin and piano played and there were dances most every night.

In 1899, the hotel was purchased and managed by George Bates, who also owned hotels in Florida. He would bring his entire staff from Florida to Mont Vernon in the early summer and return with them to his hotels in the south in the fall.

The food at the Grand was exquisite.

These grand hotels were a result of the railroad boom in the 19th century. For the first time ever, it was possible for people to travel from Boston to the country in a matter of a few hours.

Places with higher elevation like Mont Vernon or the Uncanoonics in Manchester or Jaffrey were much cooler than the city. Families would come to these places to spend the entire summer. Often the paterfamilias would stay in the city for his business during the week and come up on a Friday and take the train back to work on Monday.

What caused the demise of these resort hotels was the automobile. After World War I, cars became cheap and, instead of spending the summer in one place, people began to tour.

Tourists didn't need all the amenities; they made their own entertainment. They just needed a place to sleep. That gave rise to the roadside cabin parks and later the motels.

By 1930, the Grand Hotel was abandoned and the furniture sold off. On September 1, a great thunder storm rolled over the mountain, and the hotel burned to the ground. The way it was built, of wood with a hollow center, guaranteed a spectacular fire. The blaze on the top of the hill was seen from a hundred miles away.

The official cause of the fire was lightning, but the residents of Mont Vernon knew better.

At least no one was hurt.

But an era ended that night. ✒

Miller State Park

ON JUNE 22, 1892, some 3,000 people crowded the summit on Pac Monadnock Mountain.

They were here to hear a speech and witness the dedication of the first state park in New Hampshire. It was to be called Miller State Park.

The speaker that day was Governor Hiram Americus Tuttle.

Governor Tuttle was the great-grandson of General James Miller, the hero of the Battle of Lundy's Lane in the War of 1812. For his heroism in that battle, the general had received a gold medal from the United States Congress. Daniel Webster himself presented it to him.

In his old age, General Miller retired to his farm in Temple. The house exists to this day.

As Pac Monadnock Mountain is half in Peterborough and half in Temple, it was fitting that the park be named for the general.

That year a hotel had been built halfway up the 1.3-mile road to the summit. It was called the Pioneer House. A grand banquet was held at the Pioneer House after the ceremonies. The Pioneer House burned four years later and was replaced by a much smaller building which also burned in 1924.

The road to the summit was, of course, dirt. The road was much improved in 1936 by the Federal Civilian Conservation Corps. In 1939, the Corps built a fire tower atop the mountain, which is, by the way, about 2,300 feet high.

On that day in 1892, more than 700 horses and carriages made the trek up the summit for the ceremonies.

My grandmother and grandfather were among them in a stylish little carriage pulled by a high strutting little black gelding called Jim. It was a day my grandmother remembered the rest of her life.

She was then 24 years old and grandfather was 29. Grandmother was quite lovely and Grandfather was a dandy. That day he had on a Prince Albert coat and a tall silk hat and, as they passed Governor Tuttle on the way out of the park, the governor took off his hat and bowed low to the handsome couple.

My grandmother was to retell the story many times before she died in 1976 at the age of 107. ◆

Memorial Bridge

IN 1923, MY grandfather took my father to see the opening of the Memorial Bridge in Portsmouth.

My dad spoke of the day his entire life. See, he was one of eight siblings and there were few times that his dad could do anything alone with just one of his kids.

So when I was growing up, we never passed the bridge without Dad telling of the great opening.

Eileen Foley, who later became mayor of Portsmouth, cut the ribbon at the opening day ceremonies. She was just five years old then. Seventy-five years later, in 1998, they rededicated the bridge and Ms. Foley was again there.

The bridge was a tribute to the men who died in World War I, the war to end all wars.

It took a couple years to build the span and some of the logistics are interesting.

Each of the spans was constructed off-site and floated on a barge to the place it would finally be. When the tide was high, the builders floated the section to its final location and then they waited for the tide to go out. It did, and each section settled in place like a key in a lock.

Pretty neat. ❧

Armistice Day

IT WAS 1943, right in the middle of World War II. It was Armistice Day, the eleventh hour of the eleventh day of the eleventh month.

I was seven years old, in Miss Miller's second grade class at Milford Elementary School.

An assembly had been called so members of the American Legion could come and speak to the kids.

The Legionnaires were all men too old to be fighting in the new war. Most had thick waists and they wore funny blue hats. They were, of course, World War I veterans.

They marched in with the flag. There was a prayer and then, with quavering tones, they told us about their war, "the war to end all wars." They explained how it concluded with an armistice, a cease fire, and how it was all worth it because we were free.

Then at eleven o'clock, there was a minute of silence while the town fire-whistle blew. I wondered why they called it silence when the fire-whistle was wailing.

Most of the kids in the class had no idea what all this was about; but because the teachers were so sober, and there were all these flags and marching and prayers and all, we knew it was important and that we had better behave. Also the men talked about death, and said we kids were very close to it. That it would be no time at all before we might be in uniform in a war.

Of course, as a percentage of the time we had lived, that would be more than an entire lifetime away, but to these men ten years was but a blink of the eye.

Now that I am in my dotage, I figure these guys were about twenty years younger than I am now, younger than even Vietnam vets are now. To have fought in World War I, you'd have to be about a hundred and ten years old today.

Thirty years ago, I knew hundreds of men who were in uniform in 1918, including four of my uncles. Today there are none.

I even knew a man who was in the Spanish American War.

Since then, we have had World War II, Korea, Vietnam, the Gulf War, and the wars in Afghanistan and Iraq. And, though we still have a minute of silence on the eleventh hour of the eleventh day of the eleventh month, it is not for those who rest only in Flanders Field.

Because "the war to end all wars" didn't. ✑

Grandmother Butler

THIS IS A story of my Grandmother Butler, my mother's mother. She lived up on Summer Street in Milford. She died in 1947.

She was a very sweet lady, but she was a Yankee and set in her ways. She had been brought up in North Woodstock, New Hampshire. Her maiden name was Hansen.

Back during World War II, my mother was talking with Grandmother Butler on the telephone one fall day when, suddenly, right in the middle of a sentence, Grandmother began growling and moaning and panting and the telephone went dead.

My mother panicked.

She called back at once but there was no answer. She then phoned my Uncle Ned, who had an automobile, and told him to rush right over. And Mother called her sister Emma, who taught first grade at the Milford Elementary School. Emma dropped everything and rushed on foot the half mile or so to Grandmother's house. Mother too began running across town to her mother's house.

Everyone arrived at about the same time only to find Grandmother Butler at the kitchen sink washing her dentures.

Seems she was eating a caramel while she was talking with Mother and her uppers and lowers got stuck together and she had just hung up and gone to get them unstuck.

And she was embarrassed and very angry that it seemed half the town had come to witness her humiliation. ✒

Cut Your Own Trees

WHEN I WAS a teenager in high school in Milford back in the 1950s, we had a family friend who was on the forefront of Christmas yet to come.

His name was Harry Melendy.

Harry owned lots of acreage up on Melendy Hill and he was prescient enough in 1953 to see that there could be a lot of profit in Christmas trees.

Back then, the State of New Hampshire would give free seedlings to anyone who would plant them. The state was big on reforestation then.

Well, Harry took all the spruce trees he could get and he hired a bunch of high school kids, myself and my friends and my brother Charlie and his friends, and we heeled in thousands of seedlings in the open fields up on Melendy Hill.

See, before that time, no one was raising Christmas trees. A Christmas tree was one you found in the woods when you went deer hunting and later went back and chopped it down and took it home. They were never regular in shape. Jeez, we were Yankees after all.

Well, Harry had seen the future and, sure enough, in a dozen years or so he sat out at the bottom of his field and you borrowed a saw from him and went and chopped your own tree. Did all the work yourself and paid him handsomely for it.

Nowadays, of course, we think cut-your-own Christmas trees have always been with us. But it ain't true.

Well, in 1970, my brother Charlie and his two boys, Matt and Chuck, went out to the field that Charlie himself had planted and they chopped down their own tree, and I went along with a home movie camera.

The kids are now grown, of course, and Chuck has a daughter of his own who is older today than he is in the movie. It's a slice of saved history. ☙

The Dinner Party

WHEN I WAS a little kid, I lived in Manchester in a house up on Varney Street that has been torn down.

My dad and mom rented an apartment on the second floor. Mom worked for WFEA radio as the emcee in a weekly talent show that was broadcast from the old Hotel Carpenter. Dad worked as a draftsman.

They had lots of friends in the Manchester area, and one Saturday night they had two couples over for dinner.

Earlier a friend of my dad's had come by and he and Dad had gone drinking. By the time the guests arrived, Dad was in the bag and Mother was furious. At the meal Mother served and Dad mumbled . . .

In the middle of the meal, Dad rose and announced that he was going to take a bath.

"Why?" Mother wanted to know.

"To sober up, that's why."

"You won't get sober, you will just be a clean drunk," Mother said. "Stay at the table and try not to fall in the mashed potatoes."

"Shan't," Father said. And to Mother's great displeasure he staggered to the bathroom where the guests heard water being drawn and Dad singing.

The rest of the meal was very (if you'll pardon the expression) sober.

Mother cleared the dishes and served dessert and coffee and then cleared those dishes and suggested the guests retire to the living room.

On the way down the hall, as they were passing the bathroom, Mother casually opened the door for them to look in.

And there was father dead asleep in the tub.

And also in the tub with him were all the dirty dishes.

Mother had not taken them to the sink but rather to the tub where now bits of grease and food floated around the drunken man as he snored away amid the dishes.

When he woke up, Father was chagrined and vowed never to get drunk again, a promise he did not keep, but he was much nicer from then on.

And I'm told the chicken fat made his complexion just glow. 🐟

Mute the Milford Bell

HERE'S A STORY that happened back in 1953.

Bill McGee, Gene Ciardelli and I were cruising around in my father's truck one evening when the town clock struck eleven.

The bell up there is a genuine Paul Revere bell, by the way, and is as clear-sounding today as it was when it was cast in the late 18th century.

And that was the whole point. Like Sherlock Holmes' dog that didn't bark, we had the great idea that we might wake up the entire town by causing the bell not to ring at midnight.

The question was, how do you stop a bell from ringing?

Simple.

I knew where there was an old sofa cushion with springs and stuffing. We'd sneak up to the bell tower and tie the sofa cushion on the bell clangor.

Then the noise the bell would make would at best be a kind of whump. Not a clang.

Back in those days, you could go anywhere in the town hall. Nothing was locked up.

So sure enough, we got all the way to the tower.

There our flashlight lit up the biggest pile of pigeon guano in America.

And amid the guano was the bell.

The clangor was a hammer with a mechanical spring thingy that impelled it to hit the bell.

We tied the cushion on (duck tape hadn't been invented yet) and cruised around waiting for midnight.

Midnight came and "Clang! Clang! Clang! Clang!" . . . twelve times. Clear as . . . well, as a bell.

So we snuck back in and the cushion was still tied to the clangor.

I don't know to this day why it didn't work. We left it tied to the clangor so at least it would be a joke to someone, sometime.

Everyone agreed that, as it was my idea, it was about as stupid a thing as we ever did. ❧

Fritz the Candidate

LOOK, I AM not only an observer of the New Hampshire Primary process. I also have been a candidate myself.

I (in the immortal words of Jack Paar) kid you not.

It was 1964. I was living in Jaffrey working as a reporter at the *Monadnock Ledger*. One night I get a call from New York City. A guy with a thick, New York accent comes on the phone and informs me that he is running for president and wants me to run as his delegate from New Hampshire to represent him at the convention.

The guy's name was Marvin Kitman.

Kitman was a writer. He wrote books and also a newspaper column in *Newsday*.

He was doing this in order to write another book and also to poke some fun at the process.

Publisher Wayne Green in Peterborough had been his first choice for a representative but Wayne was on the ballot already running for vice-president.

Wayne told Marvin his guy was me.

I was delighted. It would cost me nothing and I would have to do nothing.

And so I placed my name on the ballot as a delegate-at-large, to represent Marvin Kitman for President.

I was the only man in America pledged to vote for him.

And so it went. Marvin Kitman's campaign slogan was, "I will go to New Hampshire." That was a play on Eisenhower's campaign slogan of 1956, which was "I will go to Korea."

Eisenhower was speaking of ending the war. Kitman was speaking of skiing.

As he was a writer, Marvin Kitman also had a second slogan which was, "I would rather be President than write."

Well, the primary night came and, as you probably have guessed, Marvin Kitman and Fritz Wetherbee did not win. In fact, we got the fewest votes in primary history. I think, twelve.

But I did hear Johnny Carson say my name one night in his

monologue and it was thrilling. Johnny said he didn't believe either name . . . Marvin Kitman or Fritz Wetherbee.

I was thrilled.

Later Marvin Kitman wrote an article in the old *Saturday Evening Post* where he called me "the bravest man in America."

Well, forty years have passed and I went to Marvin Kitman's website to see if he was still alive and also to find out what he's doing.

His website, I see, had this headline:

Grass-roots Movement Seeks to Draft Marvin Kitman for Presidency.

Jeez, he's at it again and he hasn't called me.

By the way, who won the primary that year?

Henry Cabot Lodge won. And he would have made a much better president than Marvin Kitman. ❧

Gregory Peck

I ONCE MADE Gregory Peck so angry he yelled at me.

True story.

Seems back in 1971, I made this 16-mm movie about early hang-gliding, and hippies and someone out at the American Film Institute in Hollywood saw it and invited me to come for an interview to be a student at the school.

It was one of those junctures that later in life you kick yourself about.

I took the invite because it was a free jet to Hollywood and free hotel, but I knew I couldn't accept the offer because of a wife and kid and no money.

Also, I had gotten a grant to make a movie over the next year and that money was certain. Relocating to the West Coast was not certain. I didn't relocate and have lived the rest of my life with some regret. Hey, tell me you don't have some similar story!

Anyhow, I got to the American Film Institute in this old mansion and there were about a hundred others there also to be interviewed including a friend of mine, Gary Anderson, from New Hampshire.

Everyone went before a panel who asked questions like:

"Can you learn more about filmmaking from books or from watching films?"

Just before I went in, this guy from New York City came out wearing this God-awful tie. So I get this idea: "I'll borrow the tie." Then when I go in everyone will think, "You know, there is something very familiar about this guy." So the guy loans me the tie and I go in.

Did the interview. Later someone who was in the hall as I went in told the panel what I had done and it played to my advantage.

Someone came up and said, "Mr. Peck can see you now."

"What?" I thought. "Who?"

My legs were like rubber. Heck, I didn't know Gregory Peck had anything to do with this operation. Hey, this was 1970 and the Film Institute was just being formed. I was about to have a one-on-one meeting with Atticus from *To Kill a Mockingbird.*

I was way over my head, and I knew it.

"Think fast, Wetherbee," I said to myself. "Have something to say."

Now Gregory Peck had just released a film entitled, "I Walk the Line," taking advantage of the Johnny Cash mega-hit.

Peck had, for the first time, played a villain. He played a corrupt country sheriff who rapes an underage girl played by Tuesday Weld . . . very unlike any part I thought he would have taken.

I decided it was bravery that prompted him to do it . . . in the spirit of, as it were, broadening his range. Later, of course, he was to play a Nazi villain in *The Boys from Brazil*.

So I walk into this huge office and down at the end is this tall, beautiful man.

I mention the movie. And Gregory Peck proceeds to tell me that these "lying sacks of chips" lead him to believe that his role was that of a protagonist. To find himself a villain Southern sheriff and a child-molester to boot was a big surprise to him and that he was suing the busters. At the end of it all, he was beet red and very angry.

I couldn't help but think it was a buffo performance. I wanted to applaud.

Instead I just sat and looked small. I wasn't about to call him "Greg" today. Heck, I wasn't even about to call him "Mr. Peck." I just wanted out.

Well, he sat there and cooled down a little. Then he told me he had seen my film and proceeded to give me an honest critique of it which I found . . . well . . . honest.

I thanked him and tiptoed out. It was not my best day.

A week later I got a call here in New Hampshire. The American Film Institute would have me if I could come.

I couldn't.

And I've kicked myself ever since. ☙

Yankee TV

I ONCE NOTED that New Hampshire Yankees never go to the dump . . . Yankees only come from the dump.

Boy, that is true, too.

My favorite Yankee story comes from Nora Sisyn. The story's about her late husband, Nick. He was, incidentally, a dear and kind friend. I do miss him.

Nick, despite his Eastern name, was a Yankee through and through.

Nick had two televisions. One sat on top of the other. In one set the audio worked; in the other set the picture worked. Together he had the quintessential Yankee TV.

My father, though, may have one-upped him. I came by one day and discovered Dad had come back from the Hancock dump with a television antenna. Not a directional antenna, mind you, but one of those old crossed things that look like coat hangers.

"Perfectly good antenna," he said.

Well, the next time I came by, Dad had gone upstairs to this kind of attic storeroom over the living room and had hung the dump antenna by a rope from a rafter. This way it could turn.

Then he took a piece of rebar (which had also come from the dump) and duck-taped it to the bottom of the old antenna and then he drilled a hole through the floor of the upstairs room clear through the ceiling of the living room.

Then he poked the rebar through the hole. Down in the living room he clamped some vice grips to the rebar and presto! He had an indoor, directional, Yankee antenna!

Worked slick as heck.

Made me wish he had Nick Sisyn's TV array to go with it.

'Course people right off hit their forehead on the vice grips sticking down in the living room just where they came through the door. Fifty percent of the time he was able to warn them in time though.

So Dad then hung a bunch of Day-Glo yarn off the vice grips so people would take notice. They did. Usually after they hit their heads though. Years later, I had a directional antenna installed on his roof and the old one from the dump taken back.

The new one got all sorts of new channels, but Dad missed the old one.

Lately, I really miss my Dad. ❧

If you enjoyed this book, you will also enjoy

PLAIDSWEDE PUBLISHING
www.plaidswede.com
ISBN 978-0-9755216-5-6 / $19.95